Microprocessor Software Engineering
Concepts Series

SYSTEM ARCHITECTURE

John Zarrella

MICROCOMPUTER APPLICATIONS
P.O. Box E, Suisun City, California 94585

Copyright ©1980 by MICROCOMPUTER APPLICATIONS

All rights reserved. No part of this publication may be reproduced, stored in a retrieval system, or transmitted, in any form or by any means - electronic, mechanical, photocopying, recording, or otherwise - without the prior written permission of the publisher.

Library of Congress Cataloging in Publication Data

Zarrella, John.
   System architecture.

   (Microprocessor software engineering concepts series ; v. 8)
     Bibliography: p.
     Includes index.
     1. Computer architecture. 2. Microcomputers.
I. Title. II. Series.
QA76.9.A73Z37   621.3819'52   80-82932
ISBN 0-935230-02-5

Printed in the United States of America

10 9 8 7 6 5 4 3 2 1

CONTENTS

	Preface	v
	Acknowledgements	vii
1	Introduction	1
2	Architecture Overview	9
3	Programs and Data	19
4	Processors, Representations, and Structures	39
5	Addressing and Memory Subsystems	59
6	System Control and Communications	79
7	Serial, Parallel, and Distributed Processing	101
8	Memory and Resource Access and Protection	117
9	Input and Output	135
10	Microprogramming	149
11	Error Detection and Correction	163

APPENDICES

A	Glossary of System Architecture Terms	175
B	References	225
	Index	227

PREFACE

Increased investment in computer design is quickly leading users and engineers alike to a new crisis point. Ideas that were not long ago experimental novelties in computer science laboratories are now being cast in silicon at a frightening rate. Just a few years ago, object and capability-based addressing were little known concepts; segmentation and paging, incorporated in the memory management features of most 16-bit microprocessors, were reserved for large mainframes.

Today, many people are finding it extremely difficult, if not impossible, to keep up with the latest architectural advances. This book is intended to serve as an introduction to the topic of advanced computer design. By integrating software engineering and computer architecture concepts, this book should also demonstrate the influence that architecture has on software cost, quality, reliability, and maintainability. In a like manner, ease of software generation and software reliability will have a profound impact on future architectural designs.

Chapters 1 through 4 introduce computer architecture and the concepts of programs, data representations, data elements, and data structures. Chapters 5 and 6 introduce the concepts of addressing and system software and hardware communication. Chapters 7 through 11 explore parallel processing, resource protection, I/O, microprogramming and error detection.

Of course, as in any technical field, terminology is a major stumbling block to the uninitiated who are trying to understand technical publications. In trying to reduce this confusion, this book contains an extensive glossary of terms that deals with the topics discussed in the text. In addition, terms defined in the glossary appear in **boldface** type when introduced in the text.

J.Z.

ACKNOWLEDGEMENTS

While this book does not describe the architecture of specific computer systems, most of the material contained within the book is based on actual or proposed system designs from industrial, government, or academic groups. In particular, I would like to thank Subhash Bal (National Semiconductor), Gordon Bell (Digital Equipment), Paul C. Ely (Hewlett-Packard), J. D. Feldman (Goodyear Aerospace), Tom Harrison (IBM), Jeffrey C. Kalb (Data General Corporation), and Steve Walters (Zilog) for their gracious assistance in supplying architecture information without which this book would not have been possible.

I would also like to acknowledge the generous contributions of many of my associates, in particular: Tony Stolz, Gary Lindstedt, and Ramsey Zarrella who reviewed the manuscript and offered much constructive criticism.

J.Z.

Chapter 1

Introduction

Applications	Payroll / Process Control
Operating System / High-Level Languages	PASCAL / COBOL / FORTRAN
Instruction Set	LOAD / AND / ADD
Hardware	Microprogram / Random Logic

Modern computer systems are complex information processing machines that consist of sophisticated electronic and mechanical components. Computer systems are designed to efficiently assist in the solution of information management problems. In this respect, computers represent the only machines available today that enhance the power of the human mind. Computer systems are, however, only tools, and tools are only as good as they are designed and crafted to be.

Computer **architecture** is the process of creating, designing, and implementing information processing tools. This process involves the analysis and design of computer systems and subsystems that interact with the "real world." The goal of computer architecture is the efficient and reliable processing of information. Efficiency represents more than raw processing speed; it refers to the ease of designing, expanding, modifying, and maintaining a total information processing solution. Likewise, reliability involves system safety and security as well as hardware failure rates.

Brief History

Well before the first computer system was conceived, it was recognized that tools could be fashioned to help people solve information processing problems. The abacus and the slide rule are excellent examples of early tools dedicated to the solution of numeric problems, while the file cabinet is an example of organized data storage. Regular use of these tools resulted in the specification of operational procedures (or **algorithms**) that instructed inexperienced personnel in the correct use of the tools.

At about this time mathematicians realized that the procedures for many numeric problems could be specified in such a manner that calculating machines, composed simply of gears and levers, could perform prespecified computations. Technological advances soon converted these mechanical calculators into electronic units composed of thousands of vacuum tubes. Numeric algorithms for these early electronic calculators were **hardwired** into the machines. In order to change the computational algorithm, an engineer, programmer, or technician had to physically alter the calculator unit by rewiring and reconfiguring system components.

John Von Neumann is generally credited with the design of the first generation of computer systems. Von Neumann's essential contribution to the science of computer design was the novel idea that algorithms could be stored as a series of machine instructions within an electronic system in the same manner that the data (numbers) were already stored in electronic calculating machines. The stored algorithm was referred to as the **program.** Computer systems in which the algorithms were stored electronically were appropriately named **stored program computers.**

Operation of these first generation computers was a very personal affair. Programmers and engineers physically entered data and programs though switches, patch cords, and diode matrices. Only one programmer used the machine at a time. That programmer had complete control over the computer's actions, starting and stopping the machine at will until the calculations were error-free.

The vacuum tubes in these first generation computers were soon replaced by transistors. Transistors ushered in the second generation of computers — lower cost, faster operation, and considerably more memory. Large core memories were developed, and professional software development began in earnest. **Operating systems** (collections of often used system software that permit computer systems to run efficiently) were designed and implemented. Commonly used system programs (CUSPS) were shared extensively among programmers, and high-level languages such as COBOL, FORTRAN, ALGOL, and BASIC were developed.

Introduction

During this period, other major pioneering work was performed in the areas of data addressing, data representation, and input/output processing. Index registers and virtual memory concepts were introduced in second generation systems as a means of simplifying data addressing. Both fixed point and floating point numeric representations were also invented. In addition, independent I/O processing was achieved through the use of separate I/O processors and interrupts.

Third generation computers relied heavily on semiconductor integrated circuits. Cost was again reduced dramatically, speed was improved, and semiconductor memory began to replace core. Software continued to become more important as software costs increased faster than hardware costs decreased.

Major hardware advances in third generation computers were due to the introduction of microprogramming concepts and semiconductor technology. Microprogramming eased the difficulty of processor design, while semiconductor technology lowered computing costs so dramatically that hundreds of new application areas were opened. In the software arena, the introduction of multiprogramming operating systems and time sharing systems also lowered computing costs by permitting multiple programs to efficiently share expensive system resources.

Today and Tomorrow

Computer system architecture has now entered the fourth generation. Large Scale Integration (LSI) and Very Large Scale Integration (VLSI) semiconductor technologies are again lowering the cost, miniaturizing the size, and raising the power of computer system hardware. Today, more storage is contained on a square inch of semiconductor material than was contained in a complete computer room barely 30 years ago. Every two or three years, the density of information storage and the processing power of computer devices are increased fourfold by advances in semiconductor technology.

One of the key elements of fourth generation computer system design is the microprocessor. The earliest microprocessors were stand-alone central processing units (CPUs) with a complete repertoire of arithmetic and logic processing capabilities. These units were designed to be major computer system building blocks and were supported by many other electronic devices including memories, latches, and bus controllers. As semiconductor design techniques improved, complete microprocessor systems were integrated into single-chip microcomputers. These LSI devices contain program and data memory, I/O ports, timers, and a complete processing unit on a single silicon chip. Single-chip microcomputers are used as stand-alone controllers in many industrial and commercial applications. Finally, bit slice microprocessors are oriented toward high-speed designs of customized computer systems known as **microprogrammed** systems (Chapter 10). While more expensive, these devices offer higher speed and flexibility than the other types of microprocessor units. With bit slice devices, a completely customized computer system can be designed while still benefitting from the cost and density advantages of standardized LSI semiconductor technology.

Software

Unfortunately, software technology has not kept pace with the explosive advances in hardware functionality. One of the major reasons for this state of affairs is the large conceptual gap between information contained within the computer system and information used by people to solve problems. Very few computer architectures even attempt to correlate these two sources of information. The responsibility for narrowing this gap has been left completely to software (notably the operating systems and language translators) that attempts to convert "real world" information concepts into computer concepts — usually with significant shortcomings.

Computer architects have often become enamored with the prospect of increasing computer system speed without considering the corresponding increases in software support. The result of this shortsightedness is generally unreliable software and increased software costs.

Logical and Physical Concepts

The main thrust of computer architecture over the coming years will concentrate on narrowing the gap between the logical concept of information (used by people) and the physical concept of the same information (as seen by the computer system). This gap must be narrowed in a consistent and integrated manner to permit people to view the computer system as an extension of their intellect rather than as a stubborn machine.

Architectural Features

Each computer system has its own unique architectural features. The following basic questions must be answered to review an existing computer system or to begin the design of a new system:

1) How complete and efficient is the instruction set (Chapter 3)?

2) What data types and structures are directly and indirectly supported by the hardware (Chapter 4)?

3) What memory addressing modes are supported by the system (Chapter 5)?

4) How do system components communicate (hardware and software) and how is software synchronized with external events (Chapter 6)?

5) What design techniques are used to increase system performance (Chapter 7)?

6) What hardware and software protection facilities are available (Chapter 8)?

7) How are I/O devices supported by the system (Chapter 9)?

8) How flexible (easy to upgrade and modify) is the system architecture design (Chapter 10)?

9) What error detection or correction techniques are supported in the architecture (Chapter 11)?

Chapter 2

Architecture Overview

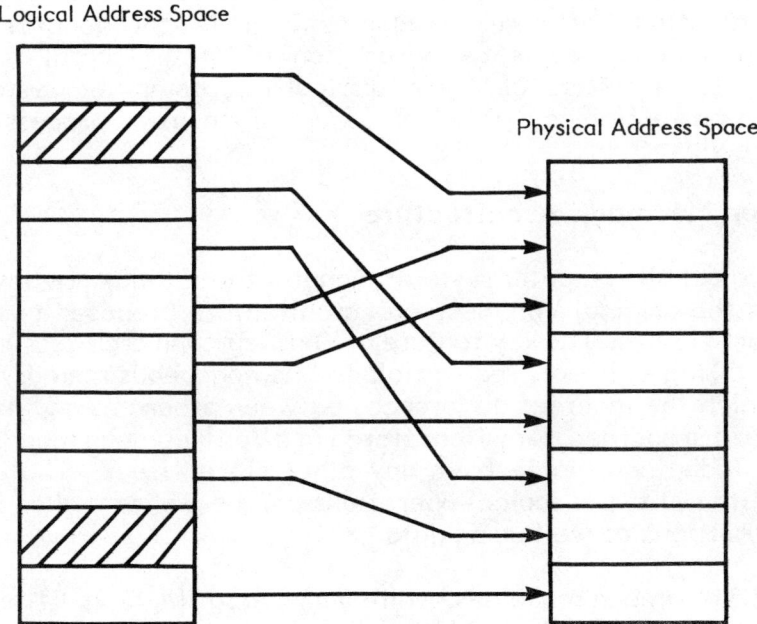

A superficial look across the spectrum of computer design illustrates that all computer systems are very similar. Each system has three major components: a central processing unit (**CPU**), memory, and input/output (**I/O**) capability. All computer systems can perform numeric computations on data, store results in memory, and output results on a CRT terminal or printer. While all systems appear to be very similar, a closer inspection of each system will reveal some very fundamental differences. These differences affect the function of machine operations, the means of accessing stored data, and the nature and extent of software support.

Many factors contribute to these architectural differences. Perhaps the most important factor concerns the methodology of software design. The process of designing efficient and reliable software is not yet well-understood. Each theory of software design has a slightly different impact on the design of the underlying machine architecture. A second important architectural factor is the difficulty of evaluating software development costs and long-term maintenance costs as a function of architectural features. Because of these difficulties, computer system design efficiency is often equated to raw processing speed.

Von Neumann Architecture

Almost all computer systems manufactured today are based on the original Von Neumann architecture proposed in the early 1940's. The key feature of Von Neumann architectures is a single, linear, sequential, and homogeneous memory in which the inherent differences between programs and data are disregarded. Any item stored in a Von Neumann machine is indistinguishable from any other stored item. That is, arithmetic and logical operations can be performed on instructions as well as on data.

Von Neumann machines, while very versatile, have little in common with high-level language constructs. For example, high-level languages assign data types (Chapter 4) to all programmer defined symbols. Type assignment is required in order to correctly select algorithms for even such a simple function as addition (e.g., adding two integers with a floating point addition algorithm will not yield correct results). A Von Neumann architecture recognizes no distinction between data types, making it difficult to map high-level languages onto the basic computer system.

In addition, many high-level languages directly support a small group of extremely useful data structures such as one dimensional vectors, multi-dimensional arrays, stacks, queues, and linked lists. These structures are foreign to many machine architectures and must be implemented in software with large overhead penalties.

Processors

A **processor** is a device that performs information processing operations. Processors contain an **Arithmetic Logic Unit (ALU)** for performing calculations, a control unit for decoding and sequencing instructions, and a small number of high-speed memory locations (**registers**) in which the results of intermediate calculations are saved.

Most processors proceed in a **serial** fashion, performing one operation at a time. Some processors, containing multiple ALUs, can perform many arithmetic calculations in parallel. These processors are used for high-speed vector and array operations. Another form of **parallel processing** occurs when more than one identical processor is included in a system. Systems with multiple processors are able to execute many programs simultaneously. **Distributed processing** is also a form of parallel processing with multiple processors. Each processor in a distributed system has dedicated memory and peripherals. Serial, parallel, and distributed processing are discussed in Chapter 7.

Processes and Tasks

The most basic computer operations are known as **instructions**. Instructions may perform simple computations (add, subtract, multiply, or divide), control data input and output, or make decisions by comparing and testing data stored within the computer system. A **program** is a sequence of instructions written to perform a specific function. A **process** or **task** is the combination of a program and its associated **context** (the information that specifies the complete state of a program). The context includes the address of the next instruction to be executed, the data in processor registers and changeable memory locations, and the processor status, and the status of all I/O devices used by the program.

Task operation (execution) is controlled by the system **scheduler** or **dispatcher**. The scheduler ensures that the correct tasks execute at the right times to guarantee reliable and efficient system operation. When a task is ready to begin execution, it is placed under control of the scheduler. If the task has just entered the system for the first time, execution begins at the task **entry point** (a point in the task predefined by the programmer). When the task subsequently stops running (while waiting for an event or because the scheduler has determined that another task must be executed), the task context is saved. When the task is later ready to resume operation, its context is restored and it is restarted by the scheduler at the exact point where it was previously stopped (the address of the next instruction saved in the context).

A **job** is a collection of cooperating tasks used to solve an information processing problem. The tasks within a job exchange commands and data by means of the communication and synchronization primitives discussed in Chapter 6. Within each task, instructions are always executed sequentially. More than one task can run concurrently (at the same time) in systems containing multiple processors or in systems supporting **multiprogramming** capabilities.

Address Spaces

As a processor executes instructions within a program, data must be read from, and written to, system memory. The specification of where this data is stored is called its **logical address**. The program's total view of memory is called its **logical address space**. On the other hand, the system hardware references a memory location by means of a **physical address**. The hardware view of memory addressing is called the **physical address space**. In many designs these address spaces are identical. Most microprocessors and many minicomputers possess identical logical and physical address spaces as shown in Figure 2-1.

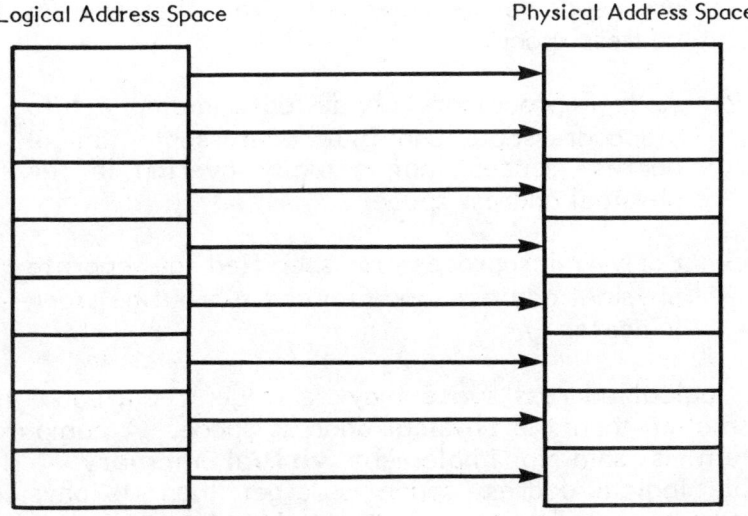

Figure 2-1 An Example of Identical Logical and Physical Address Spaces. All logical addresses are mapped directly into physical addresses.

Architecture Overview

In general, however, the logical address space as viewed by the program is mapped into the physical address space as the program executes. This mapping may be static or dynamic. Static mappings are designed into the architecture and, while easy to understand, are extremely restrictive. Dynamic mappings are performed by a combination of hardware and system software. Figure 2-2 illustrates an example of a possible logical to physical address mapping. Computer systems may implement multiple logical and physical address spaces as illustrated in the following examples:

1) Program and data memory on some single-chip microcomputers are separated into different logical and physical address spaces. It is impossible to write to the program memory space (there is no memory write instruction for this address space). Special instructions are needed to retrieve data from the program address space.

2) A few processors divide data memory into bit addressable and byte addressable logical address spaces that actually overlap in the physical address space.

3) Early microprocessors specified a separate physical address space for the subroutine stack (Chapter 3).

The logical address space may be larger than, equal to, or smaller than the physical address space. A computer system is said to implement **virtual memory** if its usable logical address space is larger than its physical address space. The name **extended addressing** or **bank switching** is often applied to system designs in which the logical address space is smaller than the physical address space. This relationship often occurs when a system is initially designed with identical logical and physical address spaces and is later expanded. Rather than changing the maximum size of a program (logical address), multiple memory banks are added (more physical memory). These additional memory banks permit more than one program to remain resident in memory. Each program can only access memory within its bank. Communication between programs in different banks occurs by means of I/O devices or special system communication facilities.

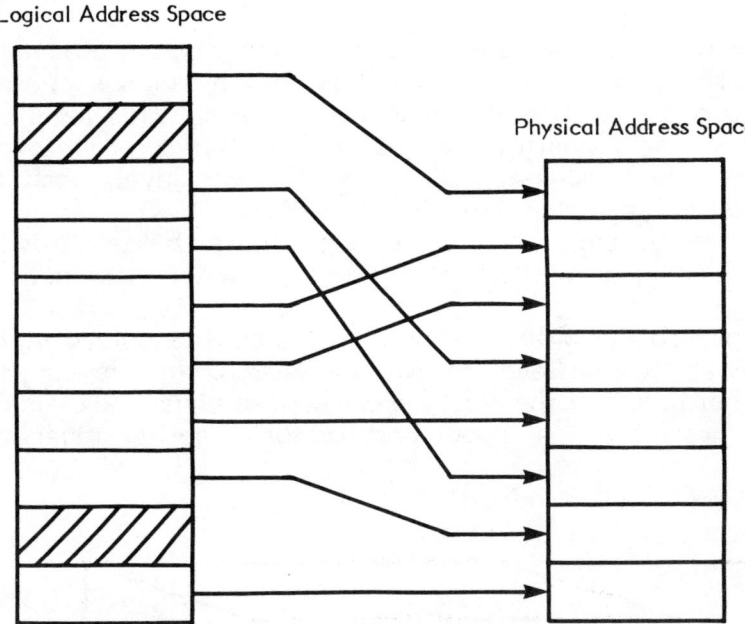

Figure 2-2   An Example of a Logical Address Space that is larger than the Physical Address Space. Each area within the logical address space may be mapped into an equal sized area within the physical address space. Note that some areas of the logical address space cannot be mapped into the physical address space (since the physical address space of the system is smaller than the logical address space).

Architecture Design Levels

Computer system architecture is definitely not a "seat of the pants" process. Many individual interface levels must be examined and specified as illustrated in Figure 2-3.

Architecture Overview   15

At the topmost level are end-user application programs. These programs ultimately represent the problem solutions that the computer system is built to support. Application programs are normally written in high-level languages such as COBOL, BASIC, FORTRAN, and PASCAL. These languages, with the addition of the operating system, define the level of computer architecture seen by the end user.

The operating system and high-level language processors interface with the computer system by means of conventional machine language instructions. This level defines the architecture as the systems programmer views the machine. On an even lower level, each instruction is implemented in terms of the physical hardware of the system. This is the level at which the hardware engineer and the microprogrammer view the machine.

In general, architecture problems should be solved at the lowest feasible level of machine design. In this way, the higher layers of the machine are kept as clean and efficient as possible. A good architectural design must not

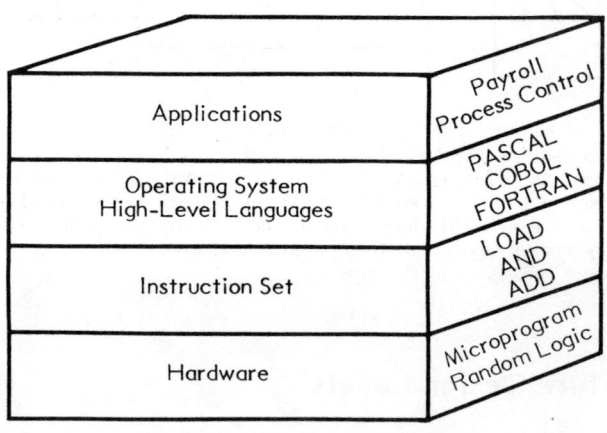

Figure 2-3   An Illustration of some Architectural Interface Levels.

only provide efficiency at each level, but it must also ensure freedom from technological constraints. If the design is free from these constraints, the speed and efficiency of the architecture will improve as the technology advances without impacting the body of software that executes on the machine.

Consistency, Uniformity, and Completeness

A computer system must be both efficient and easy to program if the system is intended to reliably solve information processing problems. A consistent and uniform architectural design is fundamental to efficient system operation and programming ease. In a consistent and uniform environment, the programmer need not be concerned about multiple mechanisms that perform the same function with many small, but unique, variations. Similar functions are specified identically by the programmer, and the system automatically and invisibly handles any special cases.

A uniform environment not only helps programmers generate software by providing simple system interfaces, but this environment also lowers long-term maintenance costs. Software generated in this environment is easier to read, understand, modify, and extend if the programs contain instructions to solve the real problems at hand and not instructions to compensate for system peculiarities.

The completeness of a computer design is a measure of the system's ability to perform all functions necessary to solve the class of problems for which it was designed. The generality of a Von Neumann architecture virtually guarantees that all desired functions can be performed (although possibly by sacrificing system efficiency). Non-Von Neumann architectures, on the other hand, may not permit certain functions to be performed. A good example is the use of read only memory (ROM) in microprocessor systems. Programs cannot write into ROM memory. This means that programs that modify themselves cannot be written for a

ROM-based system. If a function requires a program to modify itself, the function cannot be performed with this computer system.

Software Support

As mentioned earlier, architectural designs must provide efficient software support. From an examination of high-level languages it is easy to see that architectural support for the following constructs is required of all computer systems:

1) Data Types - Almost all languages in existence today provide strong typing for data. Typing capabilities (Chapter 4) allow programmers to carefully define the data that the program will operate on. With this information, the language translators perform automatic conversion when information in different representations is combined. The type information also permits the system to detect programming errors when illegal combinations of data types are attempted.

2) Data Structures - Collections of data such as vectors, arrays, stacks, queues, trees, and linked lists are used heavily by both system and application programs. New architectures are beginning to treat these data collections as unique named **objects** with well-defined access mechanisms (Chapter 4). These objects must be protected from illegal and possibly destructive access by unauthorized tasks.

3) Subroutines and Procedures - High-level languages make extensive use of subroutines and procedures to assist in the design and testing of software modules. Utilization of these procedures requires a tremendous software overhead in most existing computer systems. Only the most rudimentary subroutine linkage support (usually limited to a single instruction for saving the return address) is provided in today's computer systems.

Chapter 3

Programs and Data

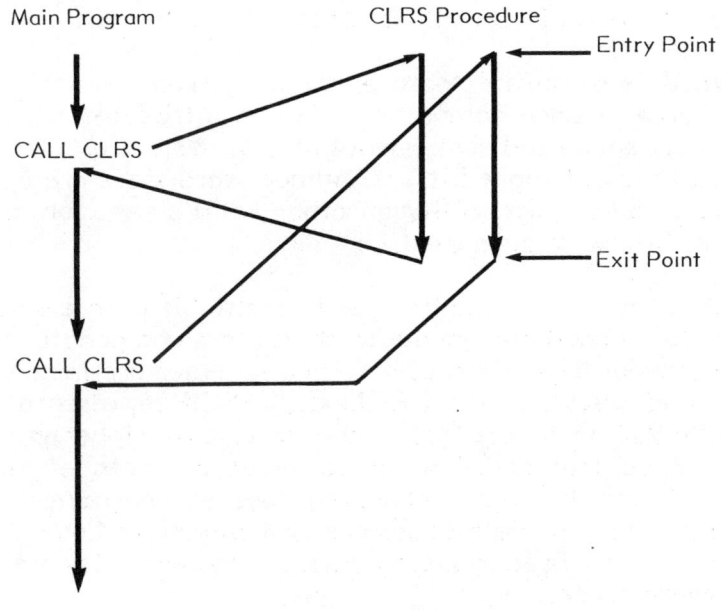

Information from the external world (e.g., employee salaries, distances between airports, or sonar contact identifications) cannot be directly entered into, and stored within, a computer system. All information must be translated into a coded physical form. The physical form of the data may be electronic, optical, chemical, or mechanical. This coded information (**data**) is processed by the computer system under the direction of a **program** (sequence of machine instructions). Although individual computer instructions are normally simple and easy to understand, programs (often composed of hundreds of thousands of instructions) can be extremely complex.

Bits, Bytes, Words, and Characters

The term **bit** is an abbreviation for binary digit. In digital systems, a bit is the smallest unit of information storage, having only two values: 0 and 1. A single bit can represent a two-state function. When multiple bits are concatenated and used to represent a single quantity, many more states may be encoded. For example, eight bits (called a **byte**) can represent 256 unique states. The concatenation of four bits is often termed a **nibble**.

A **word** is a multibit data element of fixed-length. The word size of each computer system is a tradeoff between hardware speed and cost. Generally, word sizes are defined in multiples of eight bits. Common word sizes are 8, 16, 24, 32, and 64 bits, although other word sizes such as 12 and 36 bits have been used.

Characters are typically six- to eight-bit data elements that store coded alphanumeric characters and punctuation. Two standardized character coding schemes are in general use today: **ASCII** and **EBCDIC**. ASCII representations encode 96 characters (upper and lower case alphanumeric) and 32 control codes within a seven-bit data element. EBCDIC, on the other hand, encodes 64 characters in a six-bit element. Both codes are typically stored one character per data byte in system memory to ease software and hardware processing.

Instruction Set

The machine executable specification of a computer operation is an **instruction**. The collection of valid instructions that can be executed by a processor is known as the processor's **instruction set**. Generally, instructions can be divided into six functional groups:

1) Data Transfer - Control data movement within memory, input from peripheral devices, and output to peripheral devices.

2) Arithmetic - Perform arithmetic operations such as add, subtract, multiply, and divide on stored data.

3) Logic - Perform logic operations such as AND, OR, and XOR on stored data.

4) String - Perform operations (such as search and compare) on sequences of characters stored within the system.

5) Program Control - Control program execution ny permitting instruction sequences to be repeated and by allowing the order of instruction execution to be changed based on data relationships.

6) Machine Control - Control the physical operation of the computer system by regulating processor operation and managing the processor's interaction with the environment.

In early computer systems, the instruction size was fixed by the size of the data word. If the system's word size was large, instructions often wasted valuable storage space. On the other hand, small data word sizes restricted the amount of information that could be contained in an instruction. Processing capabilities of early instruction sets were often arbitrarily limited by the system

Programs and Data

word size. Most current instruction sets utilize variable length instructions (normally in multiples of 8-bit bytes). Variable length instructions permit frequently-used instructions to be shorter than the least-used instructions in order to conserve space and to lower program memory requirements. Typically, the shortest instructions within an instruction set are data movement instructions, while the longest instructions are program control instructions.

Each machine instruction specifies the following items:

1) Operation Code - A unique code that specifies the operation to be performed.

2) Operands - Address specifications that are used by the processor to locate the data elements within the system. These data elements are processed in accordance with the specified operation code.

3) Next Instruction - Location of the next instruction to be executed by the processor when the operation associated with the current instruction has been completed.

All instructions explicitly contain an **operation code (op code)**. The operation code determines the requirements for other information in the instruction. For example, a halt instruction does not require any operands, while an add instruction requires three: the locations of the two data elements (to be added together) and the location where the result of the operation is to be stored. Figure 3-1 illustrates some typical instruction formats.

Multiaddress Instructions

The most general instruction specifies four locations (**addresses**): two operands, a result, and the next instruction. This type of instruction is frequently used in microprogrammed machine design (Chapter 10) and is

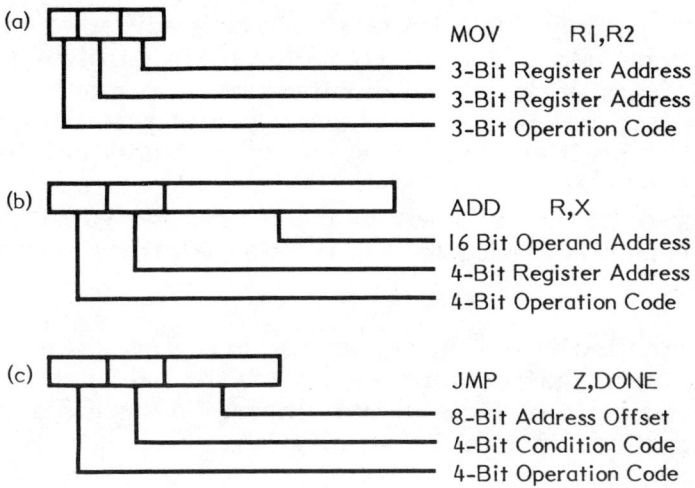

Figure 3-1 Typical Instruction Formats: (a) 8-bit data transfer instructions, (b) 24-bit direct addressing instructions, and (c) 16-bit relative branch instructions

known as a **four-address instruction.** If all instructions in the instruction set are four-address instructions, a great deal of storage is required for each instruction. An obvious memory conservation technique eliminates the necessity for specifying the address of the next instruction with the understanding that the next instruction immediately follows the current instruction in memory unless explicitly stated otherwise. In order to utilize this instruction sequencing technique, a program branch instruction is added to the instruction set and a **program counter (instruction pointer)** is implemented to maintain instruction flow. The program counter is simply incremented as instructions are executed. The program counter always points to the next instruction to be executed.

The preceding modifications convert a four-address machine into a **three-address machine.** Further instruction size reduction occurs if the result of the operation is stored back into one of the original operands.

Programs and Data

In this case, only two addresses need be specified in each instruction. Many current computer designs utilize this **two-address instruction** architecture. To make two-address instructions slightly shorter, one of the addresses normally specifies one of eight or sixteen **registers** (high-speed storage locations). Register addresses require only three or four bits within the instruction versus the 16 or more bits needed to reference an arbitrary memory location.

Some architectures reduce instructions further — to **one-address instructions** — by forcing all operations to take place in a single **accumulator.** In these designs, all operations *implicitly* specify the accumulator as one of the operands. Results of one address instructions are normally left in the accumulator. Finally, **zero address instructions** specify only an operation code. Data for instruction execution resides in predetermined processor registers or in a data stack (Chapter 4).

Machine Control Instructions

Machine control instructions are specific to the capabilities and design idiosyncrasies of a particular computer system. Most instruction sets include a no-operation or idle instruction and a halt instruction (to stop program execution until an interrupt is sensed). Other machine control instructions provide the capabilities to request interprocessor communication, to start and stop I/O processor operation, to enable or disable interrupts, to set interrupt masks, and to change operational modes.

Many machine control instructions have the ability to destroy system integrity and efficiency if used indiscriminantly. For this reason, most architectures categorize machine control instructions as **privileged instructions** and separate them from the remainder of the instruction set. Only operating system software is permitted to execute privileged instructions.

Data Manipulation Instructions

Data manipulation instructions move data within a computer system (data transfer instructions) and move data between peripheral devices and the computer system (input and output instructions). Data manipulation instructions also perform numeric and boolean computations on data. Typical data manipulation instructions are illustrated in Figure 3-2.

Data Transfer	Arithmetic	Logic
MOVE	ADD	AND
EXCH	SUB	OR
	MUL	XOR
I/O	DIV	CPL
	NEG	ROT
IN	MOD	SHL
OUT	SQRT	SHR

Figure 3-2   Typical Data Manipulation Instructions.

Unary (monadic) data manipulation instructions require only a single operand. The boolean *complement* instruction and the arithmetic *change sign* instruction are examples of unary instructions. **Binary (dyadic)** instructions such as add, subtract, and move, require two operands.

Data Types

Most current computer architectures do not recognize inherent differences among the types of data stored within the system. This homogeneous concept of storage is implicit in all Von Neumann designs. In these systems, data acquires its meaning solely through program instructions. Each instruction in the program references stored data and at the same time the instruction informs the processor how to operate on the data. Programs are free to use data in any manner. In fact, instructions

Programs and Data

themselves may be treated as data. This method of providing meaning to stored data clutters instruction sets with multiple instructions that perform the same operation (on different data types). Some current designs contain as many as fifteen unique add instructions in order to cover all possible data types. In addition, there is no system protection against illegal, erroneous, or invalid uses of data. For instance, the following software errors could occur at any time:

1) An uninitialized data value is added to a defined value. The uninitialized storage locations contain garbage, yet the processor will generate a seemingly correct result. This error typically goes undetected at the time it occurs and later causes failures in unrelated portions of the program.

2) Two numbers (with different data types) are added, subtracted, multiplied, or divided without first converting the numbers to the same data type.

3) A vector index (subscript) becomes larger than the maximum vector length. Writing data to this illegal vector element would destroy unrelated data stored near the vector.

Tagged Data

A non-Von Neumann **tagged data** architecture eliminates the difficulties associated with conventional data storage techniques by attaching **tags** to data elements. A tag specifies sufficient information about a data element to permit a processor to correctly access and operate on the element.

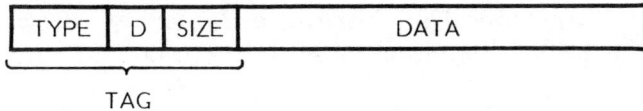

Figure 3-3   A Tagged Data Element.

A tagged element may contain the following information (illustrated in Figure 3-3):

1) Type - A code describing the element's data type. See Chapter 4 for a discussion of data types.

2) Defined - A flag indicating whether or not valid data is stored in the element.

3) Size - A code indicating the number of storage cells (bytes, words, etc.) required to store the data elements.

4) Data - Information coded according to the specifications for the appropriate data type.

Advantages and Disadvantages

The use of tagged data permits the computer system to supply a high degree of support to software design and testing. Tagged architectures permit the machine to detect many programming errors such as accessing undefined data or performing invalid operations on data. Tags also permit the system to perform automatic conversion between data types when compatible data types are combined. With fewer individual instructions, the system is easier to understand and use. A tagged architecture also increases processor speed since a simple instruction can perform conversions and vector/array operations automatically (vector operations normally require programming loops containing multiple instructions). Finally, a tagged architecture can easily permit software extensions to the specified hardware types by allowing the software to handle unimplemented type codes.

One disadvantage of a tagged architecture is the need to store additional information in memory to define data types. This factor increases system memory size and cost. However, although additional storage is required for data, instructions are shortened. For example, a system containing eight data types needs eight different add, subtract, multiply, divide and negate instructions as well as up to 56 conversion instructions for a total of 96 instructions. To encode 96 instructions, seven-bit operation codes are required. With a tagged architecture, on the other hand, there are only six instructions (add, subtract, multiply, divide, change sign, and convert). A three-bit operation code is sufficient, and each memory value requires a three-bit tag. A data reference without tags requires seven bits (in the instruction) while a reference with tags requires only six bits (three bits in the instruction and three bits in the tag). In addition, every time an instruction is coded to reference the same data value, seven additional bits of program memory storage are required without tags versus three bits with tags.

Tagged architectures are seldom implemented because of the additional storage space needed for each tag. While actual implementation is never as straightforward as the previous example, it is clear that the tradeoffs involved in tagged memory design should not be ignored.

Program Control Instructions

One of the most important features of a computer system is its ability to make decisions based on data relationships. In order to select one of two or more different functions based on the outcome of a computation, program control instructions are included in all instruction sets. Program control instructions permit the sequence of instruction execution to change either unconditionally or conditionally as the result of a test or data comparison operation. A change in the normal sequential flow of instruction execution is called a **branch.**

Conditional branch instructions also permit **looping** — the ability to repeatedly execute an instruction sequence. Program loops are utilized to perform repetitive calculations on data. For example, the addition of two n-element vectors requires n addition operations. Loops may be established to perform a set of instructions a fixed number of times (as in the vector example) or to perform the instructions until some event occurs (e.g., until the operator depresses a key).

Two techniques for conditional branch instruction implementation are prevalent today. One technique utilizes a set of processor flags (condition codes) that are set or reset by comparison and test instructions. The conditional branch instuctions simply test the flags (previously set or reset by a comparison or test instruction) and determine the next instruction to execute based on the flag settings. This method requires the execution of two instructions for a conditional branch. One instruction sets the condition codes and the other instruction checks the codes and performs the branch.

The second technique combines the compare/test and branch functions into a single instruction. Execution of one of these instructions performs the specified test and causes a direct program branch if the branch condition is satisfied.

Procedures, Subroutines, and Coroutines

There are usually many cases where similar or identical functions are needed again and again in a program. Rather than inserting the instructions to perform this function at each point within the program that the function is needed, most systems include instructions to implement **procedures.** Procedures are independent **modules** (instruction sequences). Each procedure is normally designed to perform a single function. Whenever this function must be performed, the procedure is **called** (invoked) by the program. In the example in Figure 3-4, a simple procedure (CLRS) is used to clear the CRT display screen. The program invokes the CLRS procedure whenever the CRT screen must be cleared.

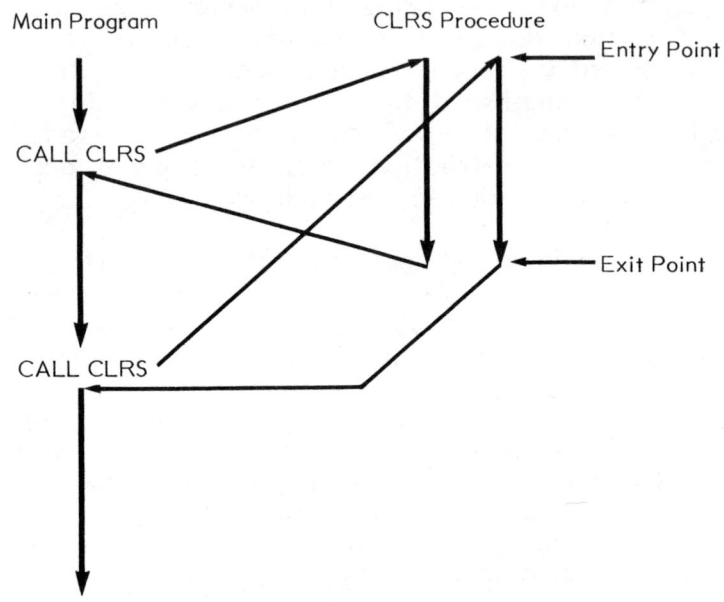

Figure 3-4   CLRS Procedure Called Twice from within the Main Program.

In general, complicated procedures require information from the **calling program**. For example, a procedure that adds two vectors may be called from several different points within a program (or even from several different programs). The vector addition procedure would not be very general purpose if it always added the same two vectors. To generalize the operation of procedures, the calling program passes **parameters (arguments)** to the procedure. In the vector addition example, three vectors might be passed to the procedure: the two vectors to be added and the vector to contain the resulting sum.

The actual instruction sequence required to call a procedure and pass the necessary parameters is the **calling sequence**. A typical procedure calling sequence proceeds as follows:

1) The call instruction is fetched and decoded by the processor.

2) The program counter (instruction pointer) is updated to point to the next instruction to be executed.

3) The contents of the program counter (address of the next instruction) are saved (in a memory location or on the stack). This address is known as the **return address**.

4) The address of the procedure is loaded into the program counter.

5) The procedure begins execution.

6) When the procedure has completed its function, it executes a return instruction.

7) The previously saved return address is reloaded into the program counter and execution resumes in the calling program at the instruction immediately following the call instruction.

A **subroutine** is a procedure with a well-defined beginning (**entry point**) and end (**exit point**). Every time a subroutine is called, execution begins at its entry point. Subroutines may call other subroutines (to perform subfunctions) and these subroutines may, in turn, call additional subroutines. The only limitation on the number of called subroutines (**nesting depth**) is the physical limitation of the memory area (e.g., stack size) in which the return addresses and parameters are stored.

At times two or more procedures are required to operate in cooperation with one another. For example, imagine an intelligent **packet switching** electronic mail system. When one user wishes to send a message to another user, the system arbitrarily packages the information into communication segments (the packets) and transmits these packets in the best manner to the specified destination. Since packets, rather than complete messages, are transferred, a destination system with eight users would receive interleaved packets as shown in Figure 3-5. In this system, the program used to receive the messages would work best if it was divided into eight cooperating procedures (one for each user).

Each of the eight procedures processes an incoming message until a new packet/user code is detected. Control is then transferred to the appropriate procedure based on the user identification information in the packet. The key difference between these **coroutines** and a subroutine is the actual transfer of control. When a subroutine is called, execution always begins at the entry point. In a coroutine, execution resumes where it left off when the coroutine transferred control to another procedure.

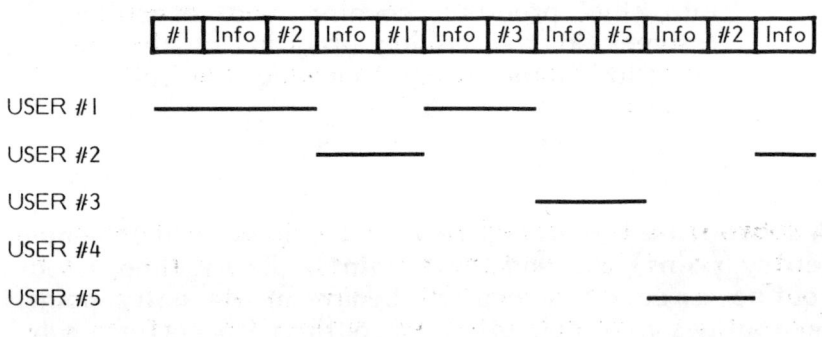

Figure 3-5　Coroutines Processing Incoming Information Packets. A coroutine accepts data until a packet header (#n) is recognized. Control then passes to the appropriate coroutine. The new coroutine begins execution where it stopped (after its previous packet).

Reentrancy and Recursion

The methods by which a procedure accesses data and saves the return address are the most critical aspects of procedure implementations. A procedure that contains its own data area can only be used by a single task at a time. If the same procedure is needed by more than one task, multiple copies of the procedure must be generated and executed by the system, wasting valuable memory space. As an example, many early computer systems saved the return address in the first location of the called procedure. If the calling program (task) was stopped before completing the execution of the procedure and another task called the same procedure, the old return address would be destroyed (written over). When the original task was subsequently restarted, it could not complete execution properly.

Modern system designs allow procedures to be **reentrant** (usable by more than one task simultaneously). To permit reentrancy, systems separate the procedure's code and data areas. The procedure data area is duplicated in the data area of each calling task, but only one code area is needed, regardless of the number of tasks using the procedure. Procedures must not change their own code areas (i.e., procedures must not be **self-modifying**).

Procedures that call themselves are known as **recursive** procedures. Recursive procedures are useful in many instances where data structures (especially trees) must be searched. In addition, many important functions are defined recursively and are most easily implemented and understood when also programmed recursively. Figure 3-6 illustrates a simple binary to decimal conversion procedure implemented recursively. Recursive procedures are implemented by storing the return address and the parameters in different memory locations for each procedure call. If the parameters and return address are not stored in different memory locations they will destroy the parameters and return address from the preceding call. Most systems utilize a **stack** (Chapter 4) to store the parameters and return addresses for procedure calls. Figure 3-7 illustrates the use of a stack in procedure calls.

```
PROCEDURE BIN_TO_DEC:

   IF N=0 THEN RETURN;
   CALL BIN_TO_DEC(N/10);
   CALL CONSOLE_OUTPUT(N MOD 10);
   RETURN;
   END BIN_TO_DEC;
```

EXAMPLE: N=231

```
                                                          Console
                                                          Output
Main Program Execution
CALL BIN_TO_DEC(231)
   ▼
   N≠0, CALL BIN_TO_DEC(231/10 = 23)
      N≠0, CALL BIN_TO_DEC(23/10 = 2)
         N≠0, CALL BIN_TO_DEC(2/10 = 0)
            N=0, RETURN
         CALL CONSOLE_OUTPUT(2 MOD 10 = 2)           2
         RETURN
      CALL CONSOLE_OUTPUT(23 MOD 10 = 3)             3
      RETURN
   CALL CONSOLE_OUTPUT(231 MOD 10 = 1)               1
   RETURN
   ▼
Continue with Main Program
```

Figure 3-6   Recursive Binary to Decimal Conversion Procedure.

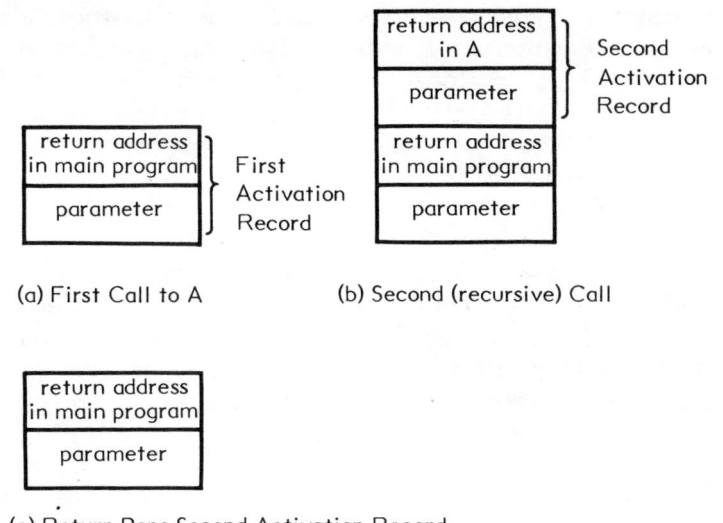

(a) First Call to A   (b) Second (recursive) Call

(c) Return Pops Second Activation Record

Figure 3-7   Stack Operation During Procedure Calls: (a) the main program calls procedure A with one parameter, (b) A calls itself recursively with one parameter, (c) A returns from the recursive call, and finally A returns to the main program, clearing the first activation record from the stack.

Instruction Coding

Each operation code within an instruction must have a unique representation in order to be decoded by the system processor. The simplest (but most wasteful) encoding technique forces the operation code to occupy the same amount of space within each instruction. The inefficiency of a fixed size encoding is illustrated by the following example. If a system requires 32 operation codes, each code can be stored in six bits. One hundred instructions in this system need 600 operation code bits. If applications of this system make heavy use of a single instruction and this instruction constitutes 50% of the code generated for the system, then the instruction coding could be changed as follows. The operation code for the heavily-used instruction is shortened to one bit; every instruction beginning with a "zero" is interpreted as this instruction. The operation codes for all other instructions are lengthened to seven bits; the first bit of these instructions is a "one" to distinguish them from the heavily-used instruction. Now, one-hundred instructions require (on the average) only 400 operation code bits (100*.5*1 + 100*.5*7).

The most efficient instruction encoding is known as **Huffman coding.** This coding requires an enumeration of all operation codes and an assignment of execution probabilities. A unique series of variable bit length codes can then be created to represent the operation codes in the most efficient manner. It is interesting to note that instruction probabilities may be generated based on static or dynamic instruction frequencies. Static probabilities ensure the most efficient use of program memory while dynamic probabilities ensure the most efficient use of bus/memory bandwidth. In practice, static and dynamic instruction frequencies are very similar.

A close approximation to the efficiency of Huffman encoding can be met with a small set of fixed operation code lengths (e.g., 2, 4, or 10 bits). While true Huffman coding has seldom been used, these approximations have been used in many architectures.

Instruction Prefixes

At times a special feature must be applied to the execution of an ordinary instruction. A typical example is a read-modify-write memory access (used to implement system communication primitives). This access must be accomplished in one bus cycle; the bus must be locked for the complete read/write cycle so that another device cannot use the bus until the cycle is finished. This bus lock can be performed with special read-modify-write instructions or with a single bus lock **instruction prefix.** Use of the bus lock instruction prefix is the most general solution since this prefix can be applied to any instruction in the instruction set.

In general, an instruction prefix applies a special condition to the execution of the following instruction. Prefixes are often used to temporarily override standard system defaults such as register bank selection and base register assignments.

Instruction Modifications

Typically, the original instruction set of a computer system is upgraded at least once during the market life of the system. When this upgrade occurs, it is advantageous to maintain complete instruction coding compatibility to the old processor while adding additional instructions. This upgrade is easily performed if there are some instruction operation codes in the old instruction set that were not used. If the number of new instructions is less than the unused operation codes, the new instructions can be directly inserted into these unused codes (Figure 3-8). When the number of new instructions is larger than the number of unused operation codes (in the original instruction set), an "escape code" technique must be used. In this technique, the processor does not attempt to decode and execute unused operation codes. Instead, the processor fetches the next byte or word from memory. This additional information is used in conjunction with the first operation code to determine which new instruction to execute (Figure 3-9).

Original Op Codes		New Op Codes	
01	MOVE		
02	Unused	02	MUL
03	ADD		
04	Unused	04	DIV
05	SUB		
06	AND		
07	Unused		
08	OR		
09	XOR		

Figure 3-8 Adding Two New Operation Codes to a Sparsely Filled Instruction Set.

Original Op Codes			New Op Codes (Floating Point)	
01	MOVE			
02	Unused	02	ESCAPE OP CODE	
03	ADD		Next Byte:	
04	Unused			
05	SUB		01	FADD
06	AND		02	FSUB
07	Unused		03	FMUL
08	OR		04	FDIV
09	XOR		05	FNEG

Figure 3-9   Adding New Operation Codes Using an "Escape" Code.

High-Level Languages

Instruction sets should be designed to enable efficient translation of high-level language constructs into machine codes. Programmers are as much as ten times more productive when using a high-level language than they are when using the machine language. By permitting high-level language constructs to be easily and efficiently implemented, the system closes the gap between the programmer's solution and the machine's implementation of that solution. When the machine responds directly to high-level language constructs, programming errors are reduced and program portability is enhanced.

Chapter 4

Processors, Representations, and Structures

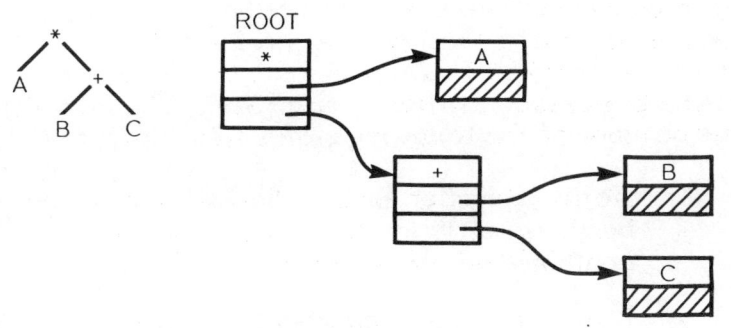

The manner in which information is coded within a computer system is called its **representation**. Processors, under program control, can decode and perform operations on data representations. Individual data elements may be combined in complex ways to form **data structures**. These structures allow data elements that have special relationships to be grouped together and treated as a single **object**. For instance, a corporation would define a data structure consisting of employees and their salaries, while a hospital might define a data structure containing patient names, room numbers, and blood types.

Processors

A processor may be thought of as an interpreter, analyzing machine instructions and translating those instructions into actions. Most processors interpret instructions in two distinct cycles: the **fetch** cycle and the **execute** cycle. These cycles are coordinated and timed by the processor's control unit. To begin the fetch cycle, the control unit requests a memory read of the next instruction (using the contents of the program counter as the memory address). When the instruction is returned, it is decoded and the execute cycle begins. During the execute cycle, the operation specified by the instruction is performed. When instruction execution is complete, the next instruction is fetched and the fetch/execute process begins anew.

As a processor executes instructions, an internal status register is constantly updated to reflect the current state of the processor. This processor status register is known as the **processor status word (PSW)**. The PSW contains one or more of the following status fields (Figure 4-1):

1) Active Register Bank - Specifies the register bank currently in use (if more than one bank is contained within the processor).

2) Instruction Set - Specifies the instruction set currently in use.

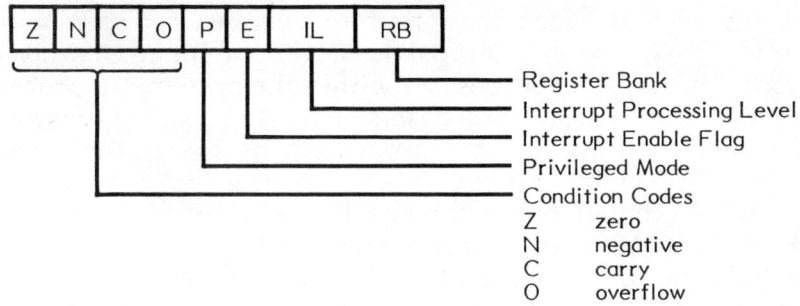

Figure 4-1   PSW Contents.

3) Privileged Status - Specifies the privilege mode of the task currently executing.

4) Condition Codes - Contains approximately four flags to specify results of data manipulation operations. These condition codes normally include flags for negative result, zero result, overflow, and carry.

5) Interrupt Status - Indicates whether interrupts are enabled. If an interrupt is currently in progress, this field also contains the service level of the interrupt.

A processor executes a **task** (serial sequence of instructions). A physical processor is often shared between tasks in a **multiprogramming** system. This sharing is accomplished by permitting one task to execute until it stops to wait for an I/O device, for an operator input, or for some other event. When the task stops, the system saves the task's state information **(context)** in order to allow it to complete execution at some later time. The system then selects another task and allows this new task to execute until it also stops. In multiprogramming systems, it is often useful to consider each task as executing on its own **virtual processor.** The state of the virtual processor (program counter, register contents, PSW, and I/O status) is stored in the task's context. The physical processors within the system are shared among the virtual processors (i.e., virtual processors are mapped into physical processors as the system executes). The virtual processor is a very powerful design concept. A virtual processor can be considerably different than the actual physical processor, offering a subset (for protection) or a superset (with software supported enhancements) of the physical processor's instruction set.

The virtual processor concept is used in many 16- and 32-bit microprocessor designs. The instruction sets for these microprocessors contain instructions that are not included on the basic processor chip. Additional devices (e.g., floating point units) may be added to the system at higher cost to execute these instructions. If the additional devices are not added, the processor cannot execute these instructions, and system software is required to simulate the instructions. In either case, the programmer sees a single unified instruction set. System performance, however, depends on the actual system hardware.

Processors perform operations on a variety of arithmetic and logic data types, including integers, fixed point and floating point numbers, logical values, strings, and pointers. Almost all current processors utilize **binary** (base two) arithmetic. Binary arithmetic is performed because electronic devices have two states (on/off). Unfortunately, humans are not comfortable in base two arithmetic. Slow, complex calculations are required to convert between decimal number representations and binary. The required conversions also have a direct impact on the arithmetic. For example, 0.60 stored as a floating point number is a repeating binary fraction (.100110011001100 . . .). On some systems this fraction is converted to 0.59999999.

Arithmetic Data

Arithmetic data is used to specify numerical quantities such as order volume, salary, distance, and speed. Operations are performed on arithmetic data by the numeric subset of the data manipulation instructions. Typically, this set includes addition, subtraction, multiplication, division, and change sign instructions. Additional instructions are provided by many processors to perform trigonometric functions (sine, cosine, and tangent), square roots, and exponential/logarithmic calculations. Arithmetic data types are typically divided into three data representations: **Integers, Fixed Point Numbers** and **Floating Point Numbers.**

Integers

The simplest representation format is an **integer.** Integers are whole numbers (no fractions). Integers count items in inventory, record population, and monitor other nondivisible items. The numbers 1, 2, 387, and 11,987,666 are integers. Integers are physically stored in one of three basic formats within a computer system (see Figure 4-2).

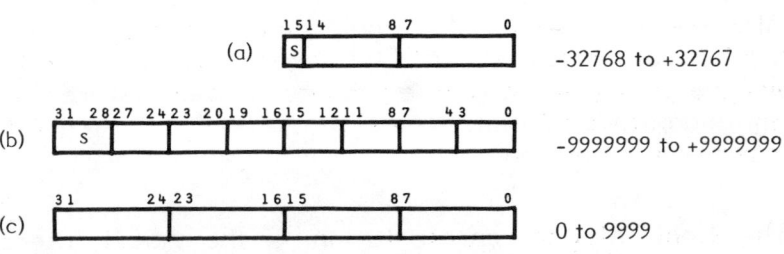

Figure 4-2   Integer Formats: (a) 16-bit signed binary integer, (b) 32-bit signed BCD integer, and (c) 32-bit unsigned ASCII integer.

Processors, Representations, and Structures

Binary integers are stored as n-bit strings. The length of the integer (n) is normally a multiple of 8 or 16 bits to agree with the machine word size. Binary integers may be signed or unsigned. The most significant bit is normally used as the sign bit. Signed binary numbers may be stored in a **sign/magnitude, ones complement,** or **twos complement** representation. Twos complement representations are used by most systems today. Ones complement has the disadvantage of two distinct representations for zero (+0 and -0). Addition and subtraction are more difficult with sign/magnitude representations. A binary integer is simply a power of two representation of a whole number (e.g., 1010 represents the number $10 = 0*32 + 0*16 + 1*8 + 0*4 + 1*2 + 0*1$). Systems with a basic word size of 8 bits normally include instructions to operate on 8- and 16-bit binary integers, while 16-bit systems include 16-bit (single precision), 32-bit (double precision), and 64-bit (quad precision) binary integers.

BCD integers are closest in format to decimal numbers. Each decimal digit (0-9) in a BCD integer is represented in 4 bits. BCD representations are less storage efficient than are binary representations. Binary integers represent 16 unique values in 4 bits while BCD numbers represent only 10 unique values. On the other hand, BCD integers need no conversion for I/O. BCD integers are often used in I/O intensive applications where only simple addition and subtraction are required. BCD integers may be signed or unsigned. Signed BCD integers are normally stored in a sign/magnitude format. The first 4 bits of the integer are reserved for the sign.

The final integer representation is the ASCII integer. In this format, each digit of the integer is stored in its original ASCII (American Standard Code for Information Interchange) I/O form. Unfortunately, while eliminating I/O conversion requirements, this format requires 8-bits of storage for each digit — twice as much as the equivalent BCD representation.

Fixed Point

Fixed point numbers are rational decimal numbers with a fixed number of decimal places to the right of the decimal point. Fixed point quantities are most useful for financial calculations where two or three decimal places are always needed. Fixed point numbers are generally stored in a BCD format similar to that shown in Figure 4-2. Processors that cannot process BCD numbers (in hardware) often implement fixed point numbers with a fixed binary point instead of a fixed decimal point.

Floating Point

Scientific calculations typically require that very large numbers be combined with very small numbers. For instance, the energy of a proton is its mass multiplied by the square of the speed of light. The proton mass is a very small number while the speed of light squared is a rather large number. The difference between these two numbers is 42 orders of magnitude. Although scientific calculations require a large dynamic range, they are typified by low accuracy (usually no more than 8-12 significant digits). The **floating point** number representation was designed to permit efficient manipulation of scientific calculations.

Floating point numbers normally have two internal representations: single (32 bits) and double (64 bits) precision. A typical floating point number format is shown in Figure 4-3. Floating point numbers may be positive or negative; the exponents may also be positive or negative. For accuracy and representational uniqueness, floating point numbers are stored in a **normalized** form. In this form, the topmost bit of the fraction (mantissa) is always set. With normalized numbers, it is customary to gain another bit of accuracy by dropping this "one" bit when the number is stored in system memory. During processor calculations the bit is replaced.

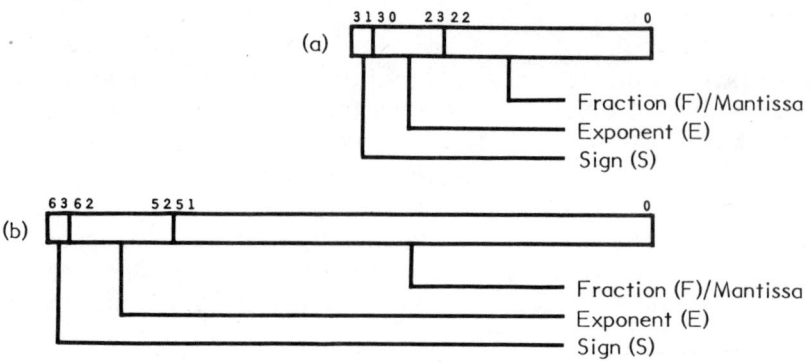

Figure 4-3   Floating Point Number Formats: (a) 32-bit single precision, and (b) 64-bit double precision.

Floating point numbers are slightly peculiar in their representations of real numbers. Very large numbers and very small numbers cannot be represented, leaving holes in real number spectrum as shown in Figure 4-4.

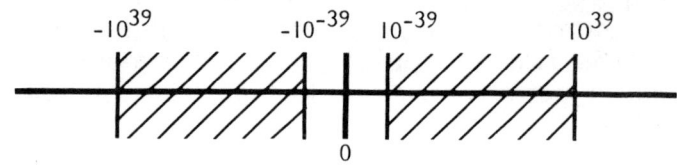

Figure 4-4   Floating Point Formats Represent only a Portion of the Real Numbers.

Logic Operations

Logic operations (also called boolean operations) involve computations on boolean (two-valued) logic elements. Boolean value are typically represented by TRUE and FALSE. The logic operations normally included in an instruction set are AND, OR, exclusive OR, and complement (Figure 4-5 illustrates operation "truth" tables).

A	B	A AND B	A OR B	A XOR B	NOT A
TRUE	TRUE	TRUE	TRUE	FALSE	FALSE
FALSE	TRUE	FALSE	TRUE	TRUE	TRUE
TRUE	FALSE	FALSE	TRUE	TRUE	
FALSE	FALSE	FALSE	FALSE	FALSE	

Figure 4-5 Logic Operation "Truth" Table for AND, OR, exclusive OR (XOR), and complement (NOT).

Boolean data representations require only a single bit (two-valued data element). Most ALUs cannot easily manipulate single-bit quantities. These ALUs use a complete byte or word to store a boolean value. Some processors, however, include bit test, bit set, and bit reset instructions in their instruction sets, permitting these processors to directly manipulate single data bits.

Strings

In the past computers were principally designed to perform arithmetic calculations. Today, computer systems perform many calculations with non-numeric data (especially in the form of text strings). Word processing and data base systems are the most well-known examples of non-numeric processing functions. Text characters are coded into binary representations within these systems. A **string** is a sequence of character codes stored sequentially in memory (Figure 4-6). Instructions are available to perform block moves (move a text string from one location to another location in memory) and to perform block searches (find a text string within another text string).

If the system word size is larger than 8 bits, more than one character can be packed into a single data word. For example, a 36-bit word could contain 5 seven-bit ASCII characters.

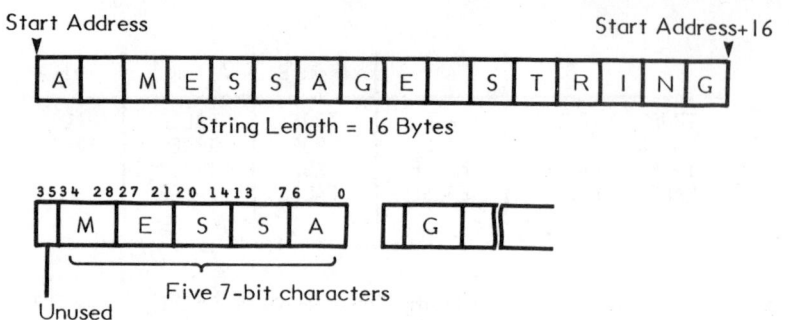

Figure 4-6   Strings Stored in Memory: (a) in sequential memory bytes and (b) packed into a 36-bit word.

Data Structures and Objects

A **data structure** is an ordered collection of information with a well-defined accessing algorithm. Operating systems, language translators, and application programs make extensive use of data structures. The most basic system data structures are linked lists, stacks, queues, vectors, arrays, and trees. These structures are described in the following paragraphs.

An **object** is a data structure whose internal storage representation is not visible to the programs accessing it. Valid operations on objects are carefully defined and tightly controlled by the system to preserve the object's integrity. Only the system can create and destroy objects. **Object-addressing** is an important concept in architectural design. With object-addressing, the programmer requiring access to an object simply specifies the object name and the operation to be performed on the object without needing an understanding of the object's physical implementation. The system is responsible for locating the requested object and verifying that the user is authorized to use the object in the manner specified. Unauthorized accesses are not permitted. Object addressing is closely related to memory and resource protection (discussed in Chapter 8).

Linked Lists

The **linked list** is one of the most powerful data structures in use today. A linked list is a flexible means of storing ordered lists of information within a computer system. Since most processed information is ordered in some manner, the linked lists are used in almost all data storage applications. In fact, because of their flexibility, linked lists are often used to implement other basic data structures such as queues, trees, and arrays.

To demonstrate a typical linked list application, imagine an alphabetical corporate customer list with over a thousand company names and addresses. The entire list is sequentially stored in computer memory. In order to add a new name to this list it is first necessary to determine where the name belongs alphabetically. All names after this point must be moved to open a memory area for the new entry. As the list grows, the addition of a new name becomes a very time consuming operation. If information could be added to, or deleted from, the ordered list without physically moving data, system efficiency would be greatly improved.

In this customer list example, a **link** can be added to each element (name/address pair). The link contains the address of the next element in the list. To move from one element to the next, the address of the next element is simply read from the link field of the current element. To insert a new element into the list (after an existing element), the contents of the existing element's link field are first copied into the new element's link field. The link field of the existing element is then changed to point to the new element by writing the address of the new element into the existing element's link field. This insert process is illustrated in Figure 4-7.

Stacks

A **stack** is a data structure that operates in the same manner as a cafeteria cup or plate dispenser. New items (data/cups) are added to the top of the existing stack and

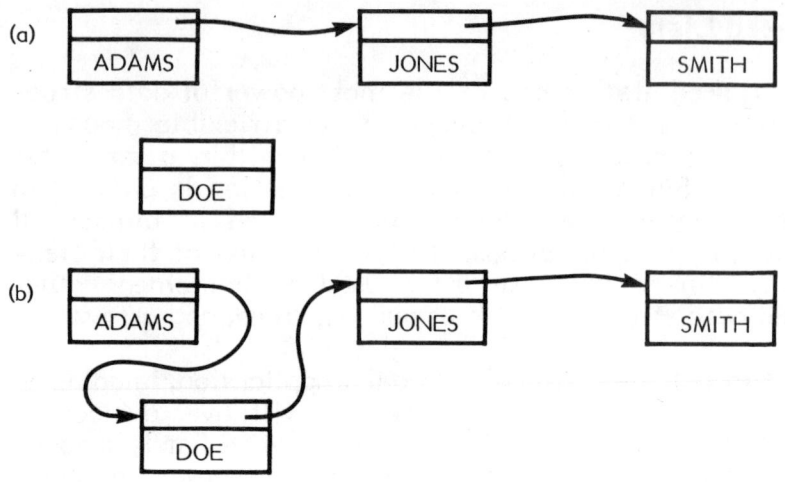

Figure 4-7 Inserting an Element into a Linked List: (a) initial list and (b) list after insertion.

old items are pushed down into the stack. Items may only be removed from, or added to, the top of the stack (all other items on the stack are "below the counter"). The last item put on the stack is always the first one off. Stacks expand and contract as data is added or removed. The operation of adding to the top of a stack is normally called "pushing data onto" the stack; removing data from the top of the stack is known as "popping data off" the stack.

Most systems implement stacks by means of a stack pointer register. This register contains the address of the current top of the stack. To push data onto the stack, the stack pointer is first incremented by one and the data is then stored in the memory location pointed to by the stack pointer. To pop data off the stack, the data is fetched from the top-of-stack memory address (in the stack pointer register). The stack pointer is then decremented by one. Push and pop operations are illustrated in Figure 4-8. In this example, the stack grows upward in memory (toward higher addresses) as items

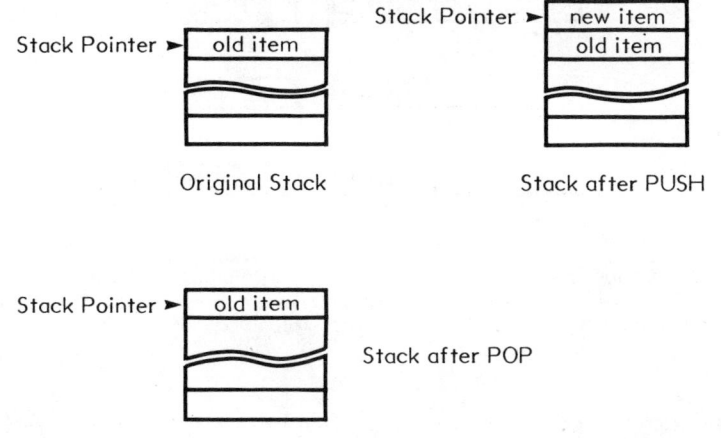

Figure 4-8   Stack Push and Pop Operations.

are added. In practice, stacks may grow in either memory direction by simply reversing the stack pointer increment and decrement operations. Some systems support stack operations with a maximum stack size limit (also stored in the stack pointer). In these systems, stack overflows can be prevented from causing damage to unprotected data above or below the stack area.

Queues

A queue is a **first-in first-out (FIFO)** data structure. A queue operates in the same manner as a supermarket checkout line or a service station line. Items are inserted into one end of the queue and removed, in order, from the opposite end of the queue. An item entered into a queue advances to the first free location in the queue. When an item is removed from the queue, all other items in the queue move forward one position (see Figure 4-9). Queues may be fixed or variable sized. Hardware queues (normally referred to as FIFOs) are always a multiple of a fixed device size. Hardware queues operate by physically

Figure 4-9   Queue Operation. An item entered into a queue (a) advances to the first free location (b). When an item is removed from the queue, all items move forward one position (c).

moving data within the queue. Software queues normally do not move data in memory. Instead a fixed-size queue is implemented in a fixed-size ring buffer with pointers to the beginning and end of the data (Figure 4-10). Variable software queues are implemented by means of linked lists.

Queues are used in applications where a single server must perform tasks for a number of customers. Examples of queue applications are:

1) CRT I/O - Multiple tasks send messages to the console CRT. Each message must be completely output on the CRT before another message is started. Rather than forcing each program to wait until the CRT is free, each program enters its message in a memory queue. A single CRT I/O task displays waiting messages (one at a time).

2) Asynchronous Operations - Two programs perform separate processing tasks on data. The time required for an operation depends on many parameters. Although both programs statistically have equal average processing times, the actual processing times can be very different for an individual transaction. A queue between the two programs allows each program to run at its own speed.

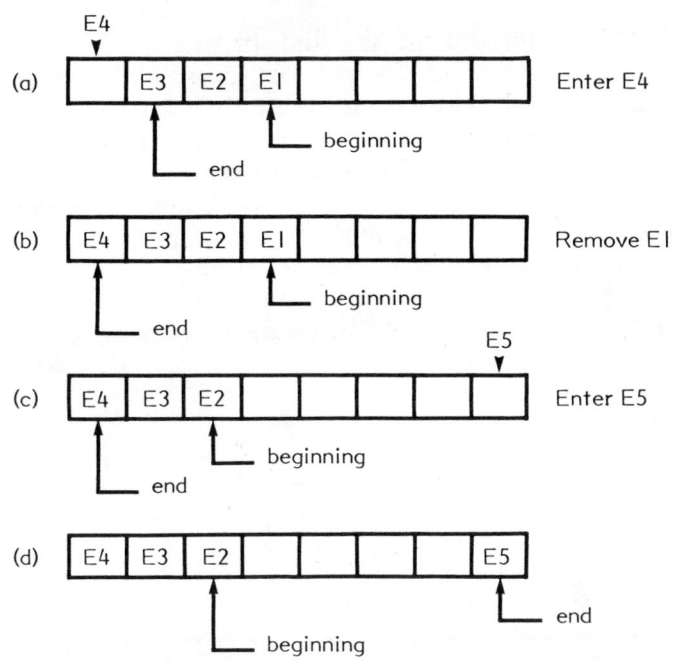

Figure 4-10 A Fixed Size Software Queue (Ring Buffer): (a) items are entered into the queue at the "end" pointer and (b) items are removed from the queue at the "beginning" pointer. Note that the pointer wraps-around to the opposite end of the queue storage area as an additional item is entered (c) - (d).

3) Disk I/O - A disk drive transfers information faster than the memory cycle time of the system. The data from each sector of the disk is entered into a fixed size FIFO. Data is extracted from the FIFO at the maximum memory bandwidth. When the FIFO is empty, the disk drive may begin transfer of the next sector.

Vectors and Arrays

Vectors and **arrays** are the simplest data structures to understand since they are similar to mathematical matrices. A vector (V) is simply an indexed list of n elements. The ith element in the list is specified as V(i). Vectors are easily accessible in most computer systems through the indexed addressing mode (Chapter 5). An array is a multidimensional data structure (a vector is a one-dimensional array). Since most computer memory is linear, arrays are translated into linear representations of their multidimensional structure (Figure 4-11). Access to arrays in a high-level language occurs as if the array was truly multidimensional. This multidimensional structure is actually simulated by software.

$$\text{(a)} \begin{pmatrix} A_{11} & A_{12} & A_{13} \\ A_{21} & A_{22} & A_{23} \\ A_{31} & A_{32} & A_{33} \end{pmatrix}$$

(b) | A_{11} | A_{21} | A_{31} | A_{12} | A_{22} | A_{32} | A_{13} | A_{23} | A_{33} |

Figure 4-11 A Mathematical Matrix (a) and its Storage in Linear Memory (b).

Trees

Information processing problems often require the use of data structures that present relationships between data. **Trees** are one of the most powerful representations of data relationships. The most familiar example of an information tree is the *family tree* (Figure 4-12). The couple at the top of the tree is known as the **root** (computer trees are always drawn upside down). Each child or couple within the tree is a **node**. Connections between nodes (**branches**) represent direct relationships (daughter, son, parent). Other relationships such as niece and nephew are implicitly specified by the tree structure.

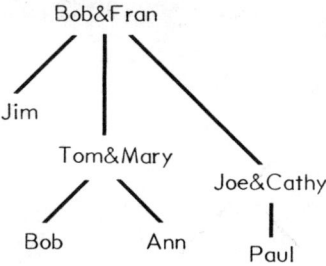

Figure 4-12 A Family Tree

Computer memory systems cannot directly store tree structures. In order to represent a tree in memory, an addressing technique similar to that for linked lists is used. Each node contains addresses of all connected nodes. From any node, addresses contained within that node specify how to travel up or down in the tree (Figure 4-13).

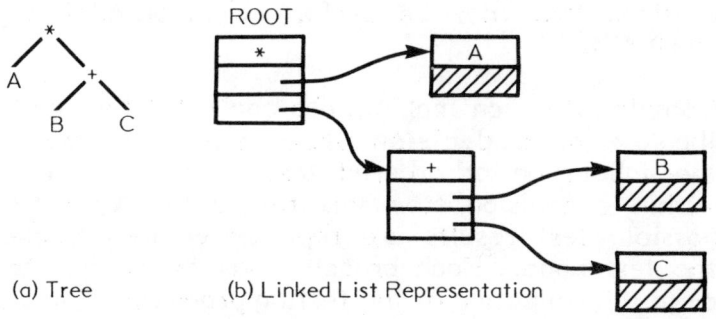

(a) Tree   (b) Linked List Representation

Figure 4-13 A Simple Tree and the Equivalent Linked List Storage Representation.

Tree structures are often used in language translators for high-level languages. In these applications, trees are used to break down complex numeric expressions into a regular structure from which instructions can easily be generated. Figure 4-14 illustrates the expression tree

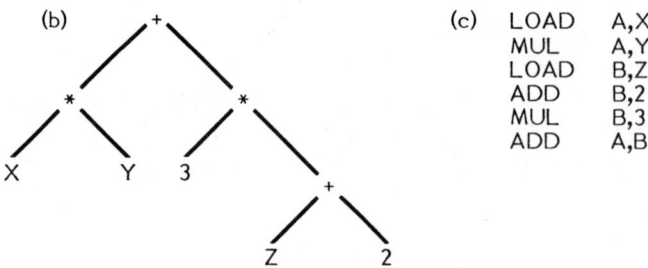

Figure 4-14 An Expression Evaluation Tree: (a) the original expression, (b) the tree representation, and (c) the resulting instruction sequence that evaluates the expression.

and instruction sequence for a simple arithmetic expression. Note that the tree shows not only the order in which the operations must be performed, but also operations that may be performed in parallel (e.g., Z+2 and X*Y).

Complex decision making jobs can often be simplified by the use of a **decision tree.** Decision trees permit the tabulation of ordered test operations. Each node within a decision tree specifies a test operation. All possible test results are represented by branches from the test node. Each branch leads to another test node or to a termination of the testing process.

Pointers

When a data element or data structure is passed as a parameter to a procedure, it is not efficient to physically move the required data into a portion of memory belonging to the procedure. Instead, a **pointer** to the data structure is passed. Basically, a pointer contains the address of a data element or a data structure.

When a pointer is used to access data, the system automatically uses the information contained in the pointer to locate the data. Pointers are used extensively in most architectures and high-level languages. In actual practice a pointer may also contain **access rights** to specify operations that may be performed on the data structure. Access rights are discussed in detail in Chapter 8.

Chapter 5

Addressing and Memory Subsystems

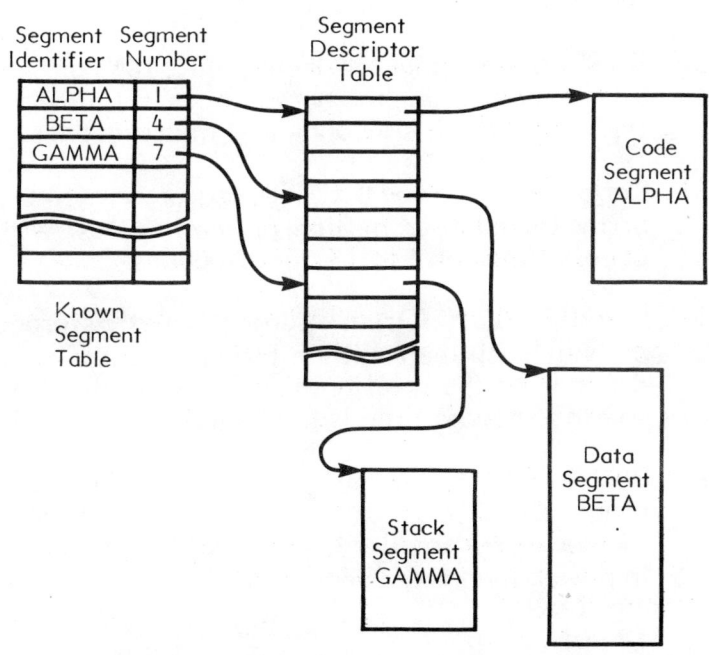

In order to process information, a computer system must access data located in system memory and on mass storage peripherals. An **address** describes the location of data within the computer system. To access information, a program presents a **logical address** to the system. A combination of hardware and software translates this logical address into the corresponding **physical address**. The physical address is sent to the memory subsystem or peripheral controller in order to complete the data access.

Memory Hierarchies

Data storage devices used within a computer system are available in a wide variety of sizes, speeds, and costs. A few common memory subsystem devices are:

1) Register - Highest speed memory (normally implemented within the physical processor). Access time may be as low as 15 nanoseconds.

2) Cache - A small very high-speed memory buffer. Access times are typically 50 to 100 nanoseconds.

3) RAM - Semiconductor devices (4K, 16K, or 64K bits/chip) or core memory. Access times are typically 150 nanoseconds to 2 microseconds.

4) Large Core Storage (LCS) - Large core memory array (often four million or more bytes) with access times of 2 to 15 microseconds.

5) Fixed Head Disk/Drum - Large magnetic storage of one to sixteen million bytes. Access time depends on the positioning of data on the disk. Average access time is 8-12 milliseconds.

6) Bubble Memory - Similar storage speed and average access time as fixed head disks. Bubble memories are smaller in physical size and lower in power than fixed head disks.

7) Moving Head Disk - Extremely large and inexpensive storage (up to one billion bytes). Access times are approximately 50 to 150 milliseconds.

Because memory costs increase dramatically with speed, many computer systems divide the physical memory subsystem into a number of performance levels. Some of these levels (disk and tape) have traditionally been treated as I/O devices while other levels (RAM and cache) have been treated directly by system hardware as main memory. A few devices (drum, fixed head disk, LCS, and bubble memory) have been treated as either I/O or main memory depending on the system implementation. The term **primary storage** (memory) specifies system memory that can be randomly addressed for single read or write transfers. **Secondary storage** refers to storage that is not randomly addressable (e.g., bubble memory), is too slow for direct access (e.g., LCS), or must be accessed in fixed-size blocks (e.g., disk).

Address Space Mapping

The division between logical and physical address spaces permits programs and tasks to be designed independent of the physical memory configuration of the computer system on which the programs and tasks will execute. This address space distinction allows invisible (to the programmer) implementation of technological advances (e.g., cache buffers). By hiding implementation constraints in this manner, physical memory subsystems may be improved without applications software impact.

The rules and data structures required to translate a logical address into the corresponding physical address are known as the **address map**. The address mapping function is performed by system hardware in coordination with operating system software.

Segments

The topic of memory addressing begins with the concept of a **segment**. A segment is a named, user-defined collection of data or instructions that functions as an independent unit. In practice, the segment is normally the basis for memory and resource protection strategies. When segments are used for protection purposes, data and instructions are segregated into segments based on the similarity of their protection requirements. In addition, segments often contain cooperating software modules. Addressing within a segment is always *relative* to the beginning (first data word or instruction) of the segment.

Static and Dynamic Relocation

When the instructions within a segment are executed or the data within a segment is read or written, the segment must occupy a position in the physical address space of the computer system. The process of fixing the position of segments within the physical address space is called **binding**. Generally, binding should be delayed as long as possible to gain the most addressing flexibility.

The earliest binding (and least flexible) is the assignment of physical addresses at language translation (assembly or compile) time. Code generated in this manner is called **absolute code**. Absolute code must be loaded at the exact location in physical memory that was initially specified by the programmer. The code cannot be moved in memory. This memory placement restriction is slightly relaxed by delaying physical address binding until load time. In order to delay binding until load time, the language translators generate instruction templates and symbolic addressing tables. This **relocatable code** is input to the **linking loader**, a program that translates the instruction templates into complete machine instructions. All memory references are modified by the loader so that they will operate correctly at the load address.

Swapping

Multiprogramming systems (e.g., real time and time sharing systems) often need to suspend and temporarily remove segments from physical memory in order to load and execute other segments. The removed segments are saved on secondary storage (disk, high-speed drum, or magnetic bubble memory). The removed segments are reloaded at some future time in order to continue executing. This **swapping** process (invisible to the user) poses problems for load time binding. When a swapped segment is reloaded into system memory, it may be extremely difficult to reload the segment at the same physical address that the segment occupied before it was swapped. Since load-time relocation is a time-consuming process, most systems use **base registers** to delay the physical address binding until execution time. The base register for each segment contains the physical base address of the segment. Addressing is performed by simply adding the instruction addresses to the contents of the base register as illustrated in Figure 5-1.

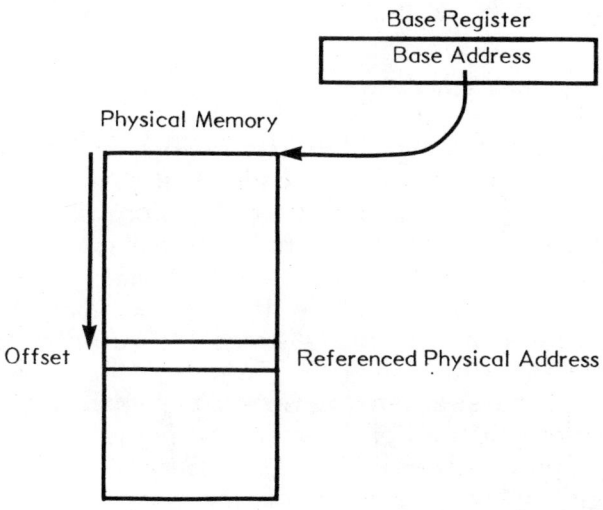

Figure 5-1   Segment Addressing Using a Base Register.

Addressing and Memory Subsystems

Segment relocation with base registers is performed by reloading the base register with a new physical address when the segment is reloaded into physical memory. When base registers are used for segment addressing, some architectures require that all instructions specify a base register for each address computation. These designs normally contain 4 to 16 base registers. Other designs implicitly determine the correct base register for use depending on the type of operand access. For instance, an instruction fetch uses the code segment base register, a stack operation uses the stack segment base register, and a data access uses the data segment base register.

Position Independent Code (PIC)

A partial solution to the run-time relocation problem has been implemented in some system designs. **Position independent code** specifies all addresses (within a segment) relative to the program counter (current instruction address). Position independent code solves addressing problems within a segment, but addressing between segments is not improved.

Logical Address Binding

If multiple segments share data and/or instructions located within another segement, one additional binding problem must be solved. As the shared segments are moved in and out of primary storage, their physical base addresses may change. Other segments that reference these swapped segments must ultimately obtain the correct physical address regardless of how many times the referenced segment is moved within memory. To obtain the correct addresses for **intersegment references,** each segment is given a unique identifier (number or name). An intersegment **(generalized)** logical address becomes a two-dimensional combination of the segment identifier and the segment offset (Figure 5-2). The system must translate the segment identifier into a segment base address.

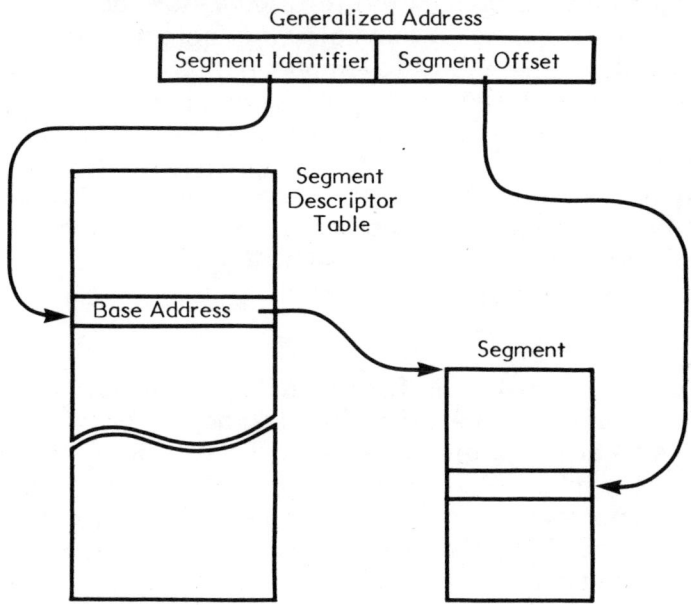

Figure 5-2 Generalized Addressing Translates the Segment Identifier into a Base Address. The segment offset is added to this base address to form the physical address.

Two mapping techniques may be used to translate the segment identifier into the segment base address. The first technique uses an extremely large logical address space. This scheme assumes that the logical address space can be made large enough so that segment identifiers of operating tasks will never conflict. With this method, each operating task references a shared code or data segment by the same unique predetermined segment number. The second method delays the logical address binding for each segment reference until the reference is executed. In this second method, each task has its own logical address space and the system allocates internal task-level segment numbers when segments are accessed for the first time. In this manner, each task that references a shared code or data segment may use a different logical address (i.e., segment number).

The first method divides the total address space into equal sized segments. As an example, the logical address might require 48 or more bits (over 300 trillion bytes of logical address space) with a maximum segment size of 64K bytes (16 bits). These sizes yield a maximum of 4 billion individual segments. Since many segments are considerably smaller than 64K bytes, it is possible to increase the maximum number of segments by permitting two or three segment sizes (e.g., small - 256 bytes, medium - 4K bytes, and large - 64K bytes).

A segment identifier is first translated into a unique segment number by looking up the segment identifier in the system's **known segment table.** To translate this unique segment number into a segment base address, another table lookup operation must be performed. This second table search uses a system-wide **segment descriptor table** that contains base addresses for all executing segments (Figure 5-3). It is impossible to directly transform a segment number into a segment base address. Standard table search methods such as hashing algorithms can be used to speed up these searches.

In the second logical addressing method, each task contains its own known segment table and a segment descriptor table. The known segment table, which contains an entry for each segment being used by the task, matches segment identifiers with task-level segment numbers (Figure 5-4). This task-level segment number (found in the known segment table) is used as an index into the segment descriptor table; no additional table lookup operations are required. In addition to these two task tables, each segment has an associated **linkage segment** or **access list.** This linkage segment is normally separated from its associated code or data segment because the linkage segment has different protection attributes. The linkage segment is prepared by the language translators and contains segment identifiers for each external segment to be accessed. When a task accesses a segment that is not currently entered into its known segment table, the

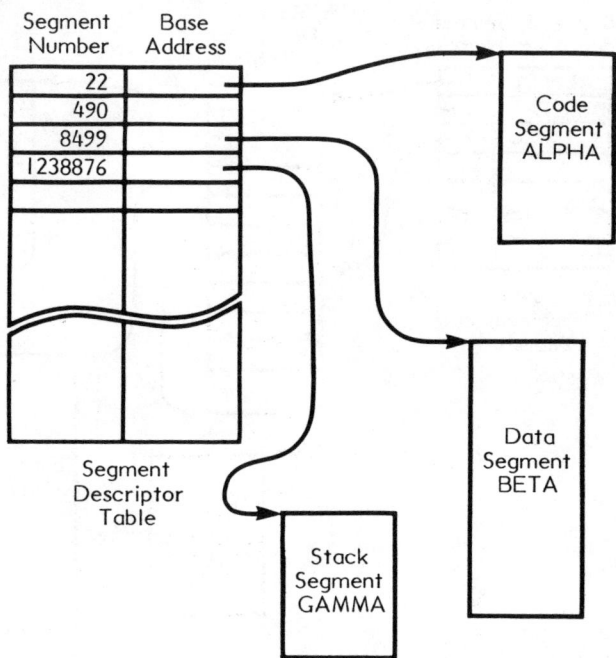

Figure 5-3   Segment Addressing with a Large Logical Address Space. The system must look up each segment number in the system-wide segment descriptor table.

associated linkage segment is used to identify the system-wide name of the referenced segment. Once the segment has been found within the system (e.g., on disk), an entry is created in the task's known segment table and in the task's segment descriptor table. All tasks have at least three segments active at any time: the current instruction (code) segment, the stack segment, and a data segment. Normally the processor contains dedicated registers for these three segment base registers (in order to decrease memory access time).

This second method provides a simple mechanism by which shared procedures can reference data from the calling task's data area and by which multiple tasks can reference shared data segments. When a shared procedure segment is invoked

Addressing and Memory Subsystems

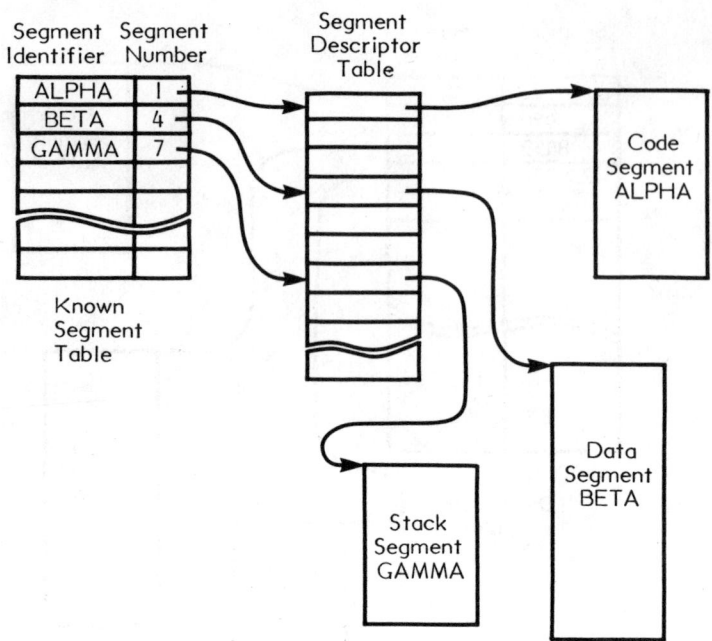

Figure 5-4   Segment Addressing in a two-dimensional Logical Address Space. Once a segment identifier has been translated into a segment number, the segment identifier is used as an index directly into the segment descriptor table.

or a shared data segment is accessed, a copy of its linkage segment is simply created and used in conjunction with the known segment table of the executing task. In this manner, references to data and/or procedures are resolved within the context of the executing task.

In both techniques, once an access path from a segment number to a physical address has been established, the segment identifier and physical address may be saved in an associative memory. Repeated accesses to the same segment use the associative memory until the segment is swapped or moved. The physical address is then declared invalid and the complete lookup sequence must occur again.

Paging

Segments are often moved in and out of memory during the execution of a task. Since segment sizes are arbitrary and segments may grow or contract during execution, a straight logical to physical address translation based on complete segments is not desirable. As illustrated in Figure 5-5, memory fragmentation results when a segment is swapped out and new segments are loaded. At some point, available contiguous memory is not large enough to load a new segment even though enough unused memory exists. When this fragmentation occurs, the system has to relocate segments within memory to provide contiguous physical space for the new segment. In addition, no segment is permitted to grow larger than the primary memory size.

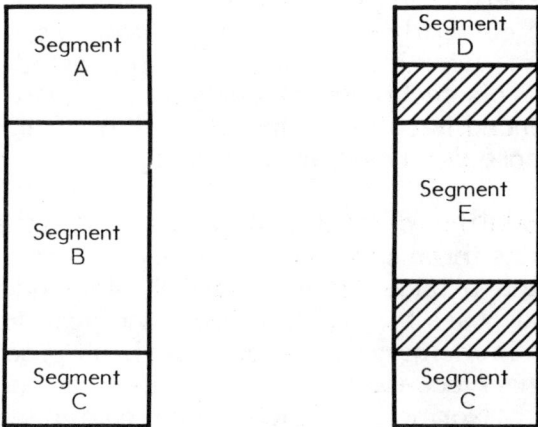

Figure 5-5   Memory Fragmentation: (a) initial memory allocation to segments A, B, and C, and (b) fragmented memory after D and E are moved into physical memory.

Paging, a physical address space management technique, was designed to solve these problems. Paging is a further refinement of the segmentation technique that divides the logical address space into **pages.** A page is normally a fixed-size block of 512 to 4096 bytes within the logical address space. Each page of logical memory corresponds to a **block** or **page frame** of physical memory that is the same size as the logical page. In a paging system, each segment is divided into pages. The segment offset address is split into two portions: the page number and the page offset. Every segment has an associated **page table** containing an entry for every page within the segment. Each page table entry contains the current physical address of the corresponding logical page. The table also contains a flag that specifies whether the corresponding page is currently residing in primary storage. When a reference is made to a page that resides in primary storage, the physical address of the reference is computed from the information contained in the page table. If the page does not reside in primary storage, the address in the page table specifies a location in secondary storage. A reference to a page that does not reside in primary storage generates a **page fault** condition. This condition causes the currently executing task to be suspended while the system attempts to load the requested page into memory. This technique of loading pages only when they are referenced is called **demand paging.** Demand paging strategies are described in Chapter 8.

With the addition of paging, a generalized system address now contains three components: a segment number, a page number, and a page offset. The physical address computation now uses the segment table and page table to find a location in memory (see Figure 5-6). In practice, these table memory accesses are not required for each memory reference. Normally a high-speed content-addressable memory contains the addresses of recently referenced segment and page numbers. In this manner physical addresses can be immediately computed. If a page or segment is moved, the physical address in the content-addressable memory is marked invalid and the next reference must perform the complete sequence of table lookups to find the new physical address.

The determination of the best page size for a system implementation is a tradeoff between the size of the page tables versus the amount of unusable space within a page. Since

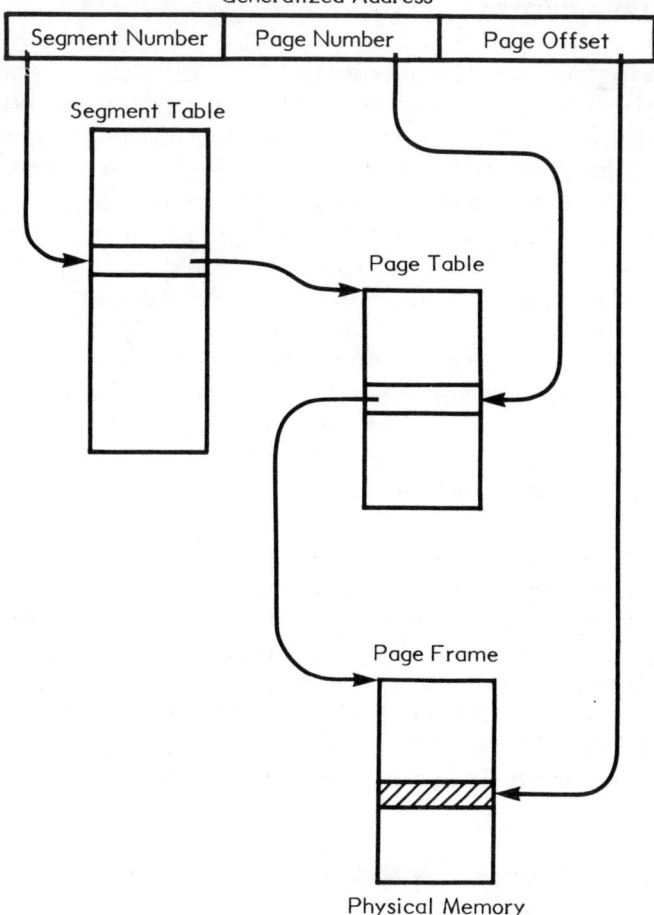

Figure 5-6   Segmentation with paging. A page table within each segment supplies the physical base address.

the last page of a segment is normally only partially filled, a large page size can waste a considerable amount of memory. Memory is also wasted if the system contains many small segments. If, on the other hand, small page sizes are used, memory overhead (required to store page tables) increases. In any case, the page size should be a multiple of the secondary storage block size. Most architectures utilize 512- or 1024-byte pages.

Effective Address

When an instruction references data, it does so by means of a logical address. Generalized logical addresses may be very large (over 48 bits in length). Forcing one or more logical addresses (in their full generality) to be coded into each instruction is wasteful. To promote efficiency, address computation shortcuts are designed into instructions. These shortcuts involve the modification of a basic logical address (stored in the instruction, in a processor register, or in the linkage segment) by data from other processor registers. The end result of an address calculation is the **effective address** of the data to be used by the instruction. The methods (designed into the processor) of computing the effective address are known as the **addressing modes** of the processor.

Normally addressing calculations affect only the segment offset (page number and page offset) of a generalized address. The segment number is independent of the addressing calculations. This addressing method in which the addressing calculation cannot affect the segment number is known as **symbolic addressing**. If the addressing calculation can carry over into the segment number, the term **linear addressing** is used.

Immediate Addressing Mode

When the data needed for an instruction is a small constant (e.g., when incrementing a register by 1, 2, or 4), it is often most memory efficient to encode the data directly into the instruction. This **immediate addressing** mode is illustrated in Figure 5-7. Instruction execution time is also shortened with this addressing mode because an additional memory read is not needed (to fetch the instruction data).

Data stored in an instruction may be signed or unsigned depending on processor design. If the data is shorter than a full word, most processors automatically perform sign extension.

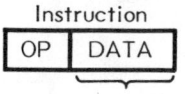

Data to be used in instructon execution

Figure 5-7   Immediate Addressing. Data contained in the instruction stream is used directly.

Some instruction sets do not have enough room to store the data directly in the instruction, but place it in the next byte or word following the instruction. In this case, the program counter is used to read the data. The program counter is automatically incremented after the data is read. This immediate addressing mode is also called **PC relative addressing.**

Direct Addressing Mode

When an address is in the same segment as the instruction referencing it, the complete address (segment offset) may be included in the instruction. This mode of addressing is known as **direct** or **absolute addressing** (since the complete address is available within the executed instruction). Direct addressing is often used in program control (e.g., JUMP) instructions.

Direct addressing is also used to address processor registers. The register address seldom requires more than four bits since the number of registers is normally small. Direct addressing is illustrated in Figure 5-8.

Indirect Addressing Mode

The **indirect addressing** mode specifies that the effective address of the instruction is not the data address. Rather, the contents of the memory location specified by the effective address *contains* the address of the data (Figure 5-9).

Many system implementations specify that a new address calculation must be performed at each level of indirection. This definition permits a program to establish chains of references within the memory subsystem (Figure 5-10).

Addressing and Memory Subsystems   73

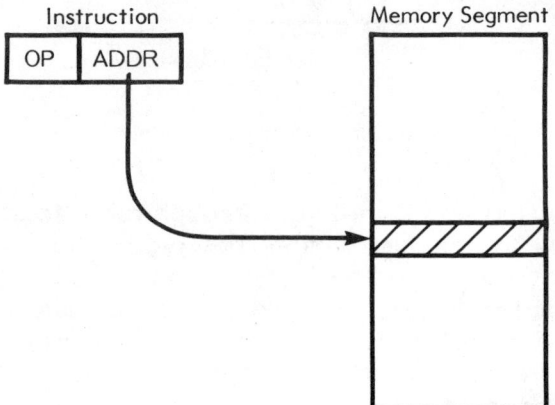

Figure 5-8 Direct Addressing. The effective address is contained in the instruction stream.

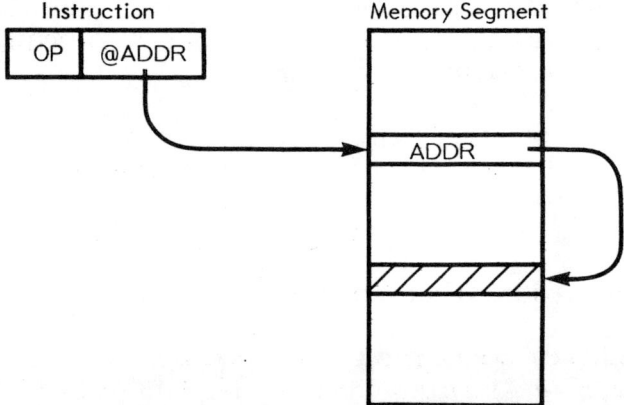

Figure 5-9 Indirect Addressing. The address in the instruction stream is actually a pointer to the effective address.

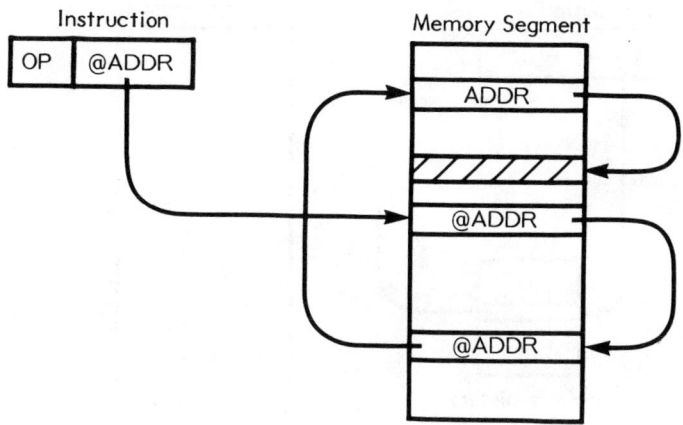

Figure 5-10 Indirect Addressing may be Chained Indefinitely in some Architectures.

Indexed Addressing Mode

Indexed addressing specifies a register or memory location whose contents are to be added to the base address contained in the instruction. The result of this addition is used as the effective address (Figure 5-11).

Combinations of indexed and indirect addressing modes can be extremely useful. The index register may be added before or after the indirect calculation. The most general method adds the index before completing each address calculation and permits the indirect address word to specify another level of indexing and/or indirection as required.

File Systems

Segments containing programs, text, and data structures must be saved, moved, and updated within the system. When not is use, these segments must reside in non-volatile secondary storage.

Addressing and Memory Subsystems

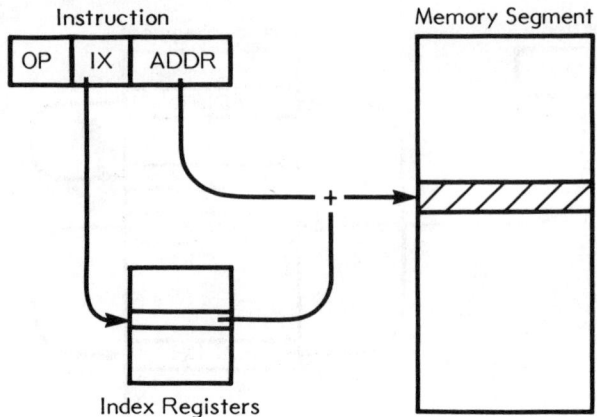

Figure 5-11   Indexed Addressing. The contents of an index register are added to the address contained within the instruction to compute the effective address.

Segments stored in secondary storage are called **files**. Each secondary storage **volume** (e.g., diskette, tape, disk pack) has an associated **directory** that lists the files existing on the volume. Each directory entry describes a file. A typical entry contains the following information:

1) File Name
2) Owner and/or Creator
3) Size
4) Address/Location on the Volume
5) Date/Time Created
6) Date/Time Last Used

In multiuser systems, volume directories may contain more than file entries; some entries may describe other directories. This type of hierarchical file structure is very flexible and can be expanded to an unlimited number of directory levels.

File Access

Two techniques may be used by executing tasks to access files. The first method treats all files as ordinary named segments. When a segment is accessed for the first time, its name is found in a directory and the segment information is entered into the known segment table. The programmer uses files in the same manner as any other data segment. This access method has been termed a **one-level store** because all storage accesses are viewed in the same manner by the programmer. The system hides the intricacies of the actual storage manipulation from the programmer. Application programs are not burdened with the problems of managing the memory subsystem (with its many peculiar storage devices).

The second method requires the programmer to be aware of the differences between files and memory resident segments. Special I/O commands or operating system services must be used to access data stored in files while normal memory reference instructions are used to access memory resident data.

Chapter 6

System Control and Communications

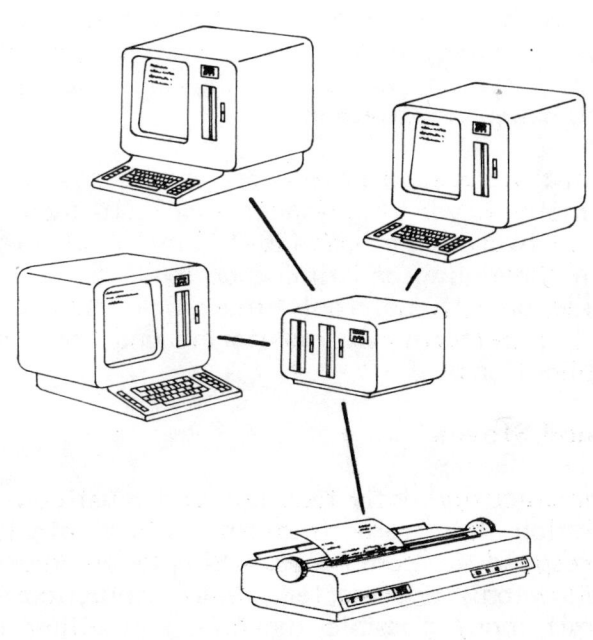

A computer system is composed of many hardware and software modules. The activities of these modules must be tightly controlled and coordinated in order to process information. System hardware components interact by means of an electrical **bus;** software components communicate and synchronize operations by means of **communication primitives** and **semaphores.** Systems communicate with peripherals over **parallel** or **serial data links,** and internal and external events are synchronized by means of **interrupts.**

System Timing

Basic system timing may be synchronous or asynchronous. In a synchronous system, a single system time base is used for all data transfers and coordination activities. Asynchronous systems require specific acknowledge signals for command and data transfer activities. While asynchronous systems permit each module to run at its own speed, these systems often experience hardware synchronization problems. These problems arise because asynchronous control signals may not meet required hardware set up times. Many asynchronous systems actually use a high-speed system clock for the critical timing of control and acknowledge signals.

The system time base used to coordinate hardware activity is normally a very high-speed clock (10 MHz to 150 MHz). A software time base (20-100 Hz) is also required for system scheduling and timing actions. Some systems also provide an optional real time clock (approximately 100 KHz) for performance monitoring and other critical timing applications.

Masters and Slaves

In all communication activities, one unit must control the communication hardware **(master)** while other units **(slaves)** respond to commands. Simple communication systems allow only one master. More sophisticated systems permit many possible masters. In either system design, only one unit may be master at a given time. Changes in mastership must be granted by either the current master or a single bus mastership resolution circuit.

Mastership may be granted in a parallel or serial fashion. Parallel resolution requires that each potential master (needing control of the communication facilities) activate a request line during a predefined portion of the system clock cycle. On the next clock cycle, a central resolution circuit interrogates the request lines and grants control to the highest priority master. Parallel resolution always requires a single clock cycle, regardless of the number of masters requesting the communication facilities. Serial resolution (**daisy chaining**), on the other hand, begins with the highest priority master. If the highest priority master needs to use the facilities, it may do so as soon as the facilities are free. If this master does not require the communication facilities, it sends a control signal to the master with the next lower priority level. This master in turn appropriates the facilities (if required) or sends a control signal to the next master. At each priority level, switching delays are introduced into the resolution chain. Serial mastership resolution is considerably slower than parallel resolution.

A master, once in control of the communication hardware, must give up control when commands and data transfers are completed. Many systems include a timeout in the resolution circuitry so that a failed master cannot remain in control of the communication hardware to the detriment of the rest of the system.

The Bus

Control and communication among hardware devices within a computer system takes place over a well-defined system **bus.** The bus is a set of electrical conductors carrying data and control information from one module (the bus **master**) to other modules (**slaves**). The system bus is often implemented by means of a printed circuit board **backplane** to which sockets are fastened. Hardware modules on other printed circuit boards are plugged into the sockets on the backplane. The combination of the backplane and mounting hardware (e.g., card guides) is known as a **card cage**.

Microcomputer systems often utilize a single bus over which all memory and I/O interactions take place. With high-speed processors and I/O channels, a single bus quickly becomes bandwidth limited. Larger systems provide additional paths from I/O devices to **multiported** memories. In addition, I/O channels and I/O processors often control their own I/O bus to which peripheral devices (such as terminals, printers, and disk drives) are attached.

Bus Signals

The signals on a typical bus can be divided into the following groups:

1) Data Path - The portion of the bus that carries data (normally in multiples of 8 bits) between system modules.

2) Address Path - The portion of the bus that carries addressing (module selection) information. A module on the bus transfers data only when it is addressed.

3) Control Path - The portion of the bus that carrries control signals and commands (e.g., read and write) to the system modules.

4) Power Distribution - The portion of the bus that supplies power to the hardware modules within the system. Voltage levels and power requirements vary from system to system. Most systems require three to six separate voltages.

The physical implementation of the bus is not always as straightforward as the functional description. Some systems divide the data path into a DATA IN bus and a DATA OUT bus. The DATA IN bus is used when the bus master reads data. The DATA OUT bus is used when the bus master writes data. This division can be advantageous if simultaneous use can be made of each data path. Most systems conserve backplane conductors, connector costs, and board area by implementing a bidirectional data bus with single-chip three-state data transceivers.

Multiplexing

Address and data information may be transmitted over the same set of conductors if certain rules are followed. In most systems the data bus is idle while the address is set up on the address bus. A specified time after the address has stabilized, data is gated onto the data bus. These two bus paths can be combined by adding an ADDRESS VALID signal to the bus. The combined address/data bus functions as shown in Figure 6-1.

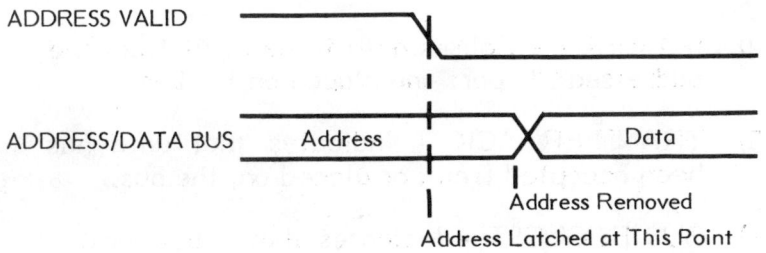

Figure 6-1   A Time Multiplexed Address and Data Bus.

At the beginning of a data transfer, the address is gated onto the bus. After the address has stabilized, the ADDRESS VALID signal is activated. At this point each hardware module has a specified period of time to interrogate the address to determine if the module has been addressed and latch (save) the address, if necessary, for future processing. The address is then removed from the bus and the same bus conductors are used for the subsequent read or write data transfer. This method of combining the address and data bus is known as **time multiplexing.**

Control Signals

Control signals on the bus transmit both command and timing information between system modules. As timing signals, these control lines indicate the validity of data and address information; as command signals, they specify the operations to be performed.

1) MEMORY WRITE - Causes data on the bus to be written into the addressed location.

2) MEMORY READ - Causes data to be read from the addressed data location and placed on the bus.

3) I/O WRITE - Causes data on the bus to be output to the addressed I/O port.

4) I/O READ - Causes data to be input from the addressed I/O port and placed on the bus.

5) TRANSFER ACK - Indicates that data has been accepted from, or placed on, the bus.

6) BUS REQUEST - Indicates that a bus master needs to gain control of the bus.

7) BUS GRANT - Indicates that bus mastership has been granted to the requesting module.

8) INTERRUPT REQUEST - Indicates that an interrupt is pending.

9) INTERRUPT ACK - Acknowledges that the pending interrupt has been recognized.

10) CLOCK - Controls synchronous system timing operations.

11) RESET - Initializes all modules.

Actual control signals are specific to the particular bus implementation. In some cases additional signals may be required to implement various functions; in other cases, signals may be combined. For example, one popular system implementation combines memory and I/O commands. All data reads and writes are treated identically on the bus. The differentiation occurs in the address. A part of the physical address space is dedicated to I/O devices. Memory references to these addresses access I/O registers rather than memory locations. This addressing technique is known as **memory mapped I/O** and is discussed in Chapter 9.

Software Communication and Coordination

Software modules communicate by exchanging both commands and data through memory or secondary storage. Blocks of data and commands communicated between modules are called **messages**. The form of a message varies from one system to another. Some systems enforce architecturally specified structures on messages while others simply permit cooperating software modules to agree on the message structure. A typical message is illustrated in Figure 6-2.

A message consists of two parts: the message header and the message body. The message header contains system level information about the message and should only be modified by the operating system or by the processor hardware. The body of the message contains the commands and/or data to be transferred between software modules. Most systems permit the length of a message to be variable; message length is then dictated only by the quantity of information transmitted.

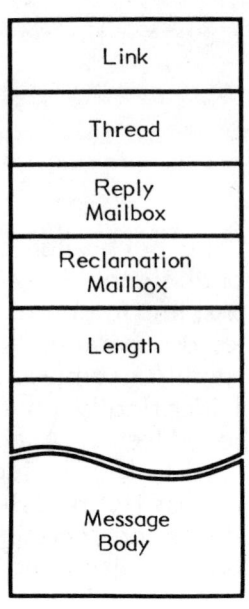

Figure 6-2   A Typical Message Format.

The message header consists of one or more of the following fields:

1) Link - Permits messages to be queued until the receiving task can process them.

2) Thread - Ties all common messages (e.g., I/O buffers) together for system error detection, debugging, or garbage collection.

3) Reply Mailbox - The location to which message replies (acknowledgements) should be sent.

4) Reclamation Mailbox - The location to which messages should be sent when the receiving task has finished processing the message. The operating system or hardware uses this location to reclaim memory space for later reuse.

5) Length - Size of the message body.

Synchronization

Data to be transferred between tasks must only be transferred when the receiving task is ready for the data, and the new data must not be allowed to invalidate previously transmitted data. For example, a new message buffer for output must not be permitted to overwrite the previous buffer until the previous buffer has been printed. This restriction is called **synchronization.**

Synchronization between tasks is implemented using **event flags, semaphores,** and **mailboxes.** Event flags are used to synchronize task operation with external events or with another task. In operation, a task waits on an event flag. When the flag is set (by an external event or another task) the system automatically passes the waiting task to the system scheduler (in order to continue execution). Event flags are not sufficient for synchronizing multiple tasks that require access to the same resources. To synchronize multiple tasks, either **semaphores** or **mailboxes** must be used.

Semaphores

A semaphore acts like a gate into a restricted area or **critical section** of software (protecting shared data or I/O). Initially the gate is open, but when the first task enters the restricted area, it automatically closes the gate to lock out any other tasks. The task within the critical section may access the shared data with the assurance that no other task will be permitted access until the current task is finished. This locking gate is implemented via two indivisible operations (P and V). The status of the gate has only two values (*open* or *closed*). When a task wishes access to shared data, it executes a P operation. This operation tests the state of the gate. If the gate is open, it is immediately closed and locked (within the same hardware instruction so that no other task may interrupt this *test and set* operation). If the gate is closed, the task may not enter the critical section and it must wait until the gate is reopened.

Once a task has gained access to shared data via the P operation, it performs the required data manipulation and exits the critical section. At this point the task executes the V operation that opens the gate and allows one and only one of the waiting tasks to enter the section. If no tasks are waiting, the gate is left open for the next task that wishes access.

Busy Wait

The only problem posed by semaphores occurs when they are totally implemented in software since in order to enter the critical region, a test of the "gate" must be made to determine whether it is open or closed. If it is closed, a task must wait until it is opened. Unless there is some hardware facility for waiting, the task must continually test this gate. Even though the task is not performing any useful work during the wait, the processor that the task is running on is busy executing test instructions that prevent any other task from executing during this time. This is called a **busy wait**.

Mailboxes

Mailboxes are a slightly different method of implementing task synchronization. When a task has data to send to another cooperating task, it places a message containing the data in a mailbox for the receiving task. This mailbox is actually a **queue** where messages are stacked. The receiving task, when it is ready, looks in the mailbox and picks up the next message. Any number of transmitting tasks can place messages in the mailbox. In order to operate correctly, three indivisible mailbox operations (**communication primitives**) are defined:

1) **send** - places a message in the appropriate mailbox.

2) **wait** - extracts a message from the appropriate mailbox. It will wait until a message arrives if the mailbox is empty. The task is suspended during this time.

3) **accept** - extracts a message from the appropriate mailbox, but does not wait if the mailbox is empty. This action allows a task to periodically check multiple mailboxes for messages.

It should be noted that when mailboxes are used, an inherent critical section is contained in the queue operations. It is imperative that addition to, or removal from, the queue is protected by a semaphore until the operation is completed.

Interrupts

All computer systems interact with the "real world." Systems receive inputs, process information, and ultimately output this processed information on terminals or printers. Input and output operations require the capability to synchronize computer operation with external events (signals). These external events are often asynchronous to system operation and may occur at any time during program execution. One means of synchronizing system software with external events is known as **polling**. To implement this technique, software periodically samples inputs and checks to see if relevant events have occurred. If the polling interval is too long, an event may happen well before it is noticed. By the time the software recognizes the event, data could be lost, damage could occur, or injury could result. On the other hand, if the polling interval is too short, valuable processor time is wasted (while performing I/O operations and testing input data) and system efficiency deteriorates.

Interrupts are designed to provide fast response to external events with low processor overhead. The concept of an interrupt is analogous to the use of the timer on an oven. After food is placed in the oven, the timer is set for the length of time required to cook the food. If the timer did not buzz when the food was done, it would have to be checked every few minutes to see if the cooking time was up. If the time between checkings (polling interval) was too long, the food could burn. The buzzer enables the cook to put food in the oven and completely forget about it. When the buzzer sounds, the cook knows that the dinner is done (regardless of other projects in progress). In the same manner, interrupts effectively let the processor ignore outside events until they happen.

Processors normally recognize interrupts at a fixed time within each instruction cycle. When an interrupt is recognized, the processor begins execution of a new software module (immediately after completing execution of the current instruction). Before beginning execution of the new software module, the context of the currently executing software module must be saved so that this module can continue execution after the interrupt has been serviced.

Most processors simply branch to an interrupt service routine at a predefined location in memory after saving the program counter (current instruction address) in memory. The remainder of the context switch (saving registers, I/O status, and processor status) must be implemented by the interrupt service software. This context switch can involve significant delays while data is stored and retrieved. Once the context switch is completed, interrupt processing is started. After interrupt processing has been completed, the context of the original software module is restored and processing is resumed at the point where the interrupt occurred.

The time delay between the occurrence of the interrupt and the beginning of interrupt processing is called **interrupt latency.** Most specifications define latency as the time between the interrupt occurrence and the beginning of the interrupt service software. This definition is misleading since it usually does not include software context switching time.

In systems where many interrupts may occur, each interrupt is normally assigned a code (e.g., 0 through 255). These systems use this interrupt code as an index into a memory resident table of interrupt service routine addresses. When an interrupt is recognized, the processor extracts the correct address from this resident table and loads the address into the program counter (after saving the previous contents of the program counter in memory). This method of interrupt processing is known as a **vectored interrupt** implementation. In these systems, interrupt priorities are established to ensure that low-priority events cannot interfere with the servicing of high-priority events. Most systems permit programmable masking of interrupt requests, permitting an executing task to inhibit interrupt servicing during critical functions. For example, this masking capability is used when it is necessary to complete a multiinstruction operation without interruption.

When an interrupt request is recognized, most architectures immediately suspend operation of the currently executing task. This technique makes it difficult to merge software task priorities and interrupt service priorities. Recent machine designs have integrated software and hardware priority resolution into the task scheduling mechanism. These designs only suspend the currently executing task when a hardware interrupt has a higher system priority.

Data Links

Data links permit computer systems to transmit information to, and receive information from, other systems over large distances. Data links may be established between systems in the same building over dedicated cables or between systems in widely separated countries by means of telephone and satellite links. Sophisticated hardware and software are required to provide reliable and error-free communication between computer systems. The term **protocol** is used to specify the rules by which messages (containing information) are transmitted between computer systems. A protocol specifies hardware requirements such as maximum and minimum line lengths, data rates, and voltage levels as well as software requirements such as maximum message length, message format, and error detection codes.

Before information can be transmitted from one system to another, hardware and software in the transmitting system must translate this information into one or more message frames (according to the applicable protocol). A typical message frame is shown in Figure 6-3. It contains the following fields:

1) Flag - A code that signifies the beginning or end of a message frame.

2) Address - Identifies the device that is to receive and process the message.

3) Information - Actual data to be transferred.

4) Error Check - A code that allows the receiver to determine if the information has been "garbled" in any way during transmission.

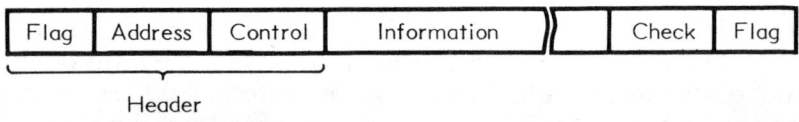

Figure 6-3   A Communications Message Frame.

Physical Transmission Characteristics

Messages are most often transmitted by means of twisted pair, coaxial, or fiber optic cables. Twisted pair cables are used only for low speeds and short distances, while coaxial and fiber optic cables are utilized for long-distance, high-speed data transmission. Information can be transmitted between systems in a **parallel** or **serial** format. Parallel transmission exchanges all data bits within a word (typically 8 or 16 bits) simultaneously (in one cycle). Serial transmission transfers one bit at a time; an 8-bit transfer requires eight transfer cycles. Parallel transmission techniques are faster than serial techniques, but the cost of cabling with the required number of conductors rules out parallel data techniques for all but the shortest distances where extremely high speed is required. For example, parallel interfaces are often used for interprocessor communication between systems contained within the same computer room.

Serial Communication

Serial data links are often used to communicate between computer systems and peripheral devices because serial data links provide flexible and low-cost I/O interfaces. Good serial protocols operate reliably at a varity of transmission rates and distances. When messages are transmitted and received by means of a serial data link, both the receiving and transmitting devices require a method of determining the beginning and end of each bit in the serial data stream. **Synchronous** communication forces both the transmitter and receiver to operate from the same clock. Bit centers are sampled in the data stream on the clock edges. This clock must normally be transmitted with the data to the receiving system. SDLC-type protocols use an ingenious scheme. By guaranteeing a transition in the data stream at least every 6 bits, a phase-locked loop can generate and maintain a synchronous clock directly from the data stream. Of course, since the transmitted data may not contain natural transitions (e.g., an all zero word), the transmitter hardware inserts extra bits into the data stream (where required) and the receiver hardware removes these bits automatically.

Asynchronous communication does not rely on synchronous clocks to separate data bits. Instead, a clock 16 to 64 times as fast as the data transmission rate is used by the receiver. Special START and STOP framing bits are included in the transmitted data. Normally the data link is in an idle condition. When a change occurs, the receiver assumes that a start bit has been received. It tests this assumption (to rule out noise) by waiting one-half bit time (8-32 clocks). If the link has returned to the idle state, the noise is ignored. Otherwise data bits are sampled at their nominal centers until all bits have been received. A STOP bit is transmitted to ensure that the character frame has ended correctly. Any time after the STOP bit, the START bit for the next character may be transmitted.

Each character is framed by a START bit and one or two STOP bits. The transmission of an 8-bit byte requires ten or eleven bits. Although asynchronous transmission is slower than synchronous transmission, no additional clocks are needed and the transmission and reception techniques are simple.

Serial data transmission between two devices can occur in one of three modes. A **simplex** transmission line can transmit in one direction only; a **half-duplex** line can transmit in both directions, but not simultaneously; and a **full-duplex** line can transmit in both directions simultaneously. When half-duplex lines are reversed, a small idle period (**line turnaround time**) is required during which data cannot be transmitted in either direction. Serial interface transmission speed is measured in bits/second. The term **baud** is used to specify the number of times per second that the transmitted signal level can change. In general, baud rate is not equal to bit rate. Only when the transmitted signal has two states (electrical levels) is the baud rate equal to the bit rate.

Parallel Communication

A popular parallel communication interface bus is the GPIB (General Purpose Instrumentation Bus), also known as the **IEEE-488** bus. This bus permits asynchronous 8-bit parallel data transfers at speeds up to one million bytes per second. Each unit on the bus has one of three possible designations: talker, listener, or controller. Each bus has one controller. Data transmission between units occurs as follows:

1) The controller selects the device that is to transmit data and places it in the talker mode.

2) The controller selects the device that is to receive the data and places it in the listener mode.

3) The controller initiates data transmission.

4) The talker and listener transfer data: the talker places and holds a data byte on the bus; the listener signals acceptance when it has received the data; and the talker then proceeds to place another byte on the bus.

5) After all data is transferred, the controller begins a new information transfer.

Networks

A data communication system consisting of multiple computer systems and data links is referred to as a communication **network**. Systems (**nodes**) may be connected to the network data links in a variety of configurations:

1) **Star** - All devices are connected to a single network master. Communication lines emanate from this unit in a star-like shape (Figure 6-4). Each device communicates only with the network master.

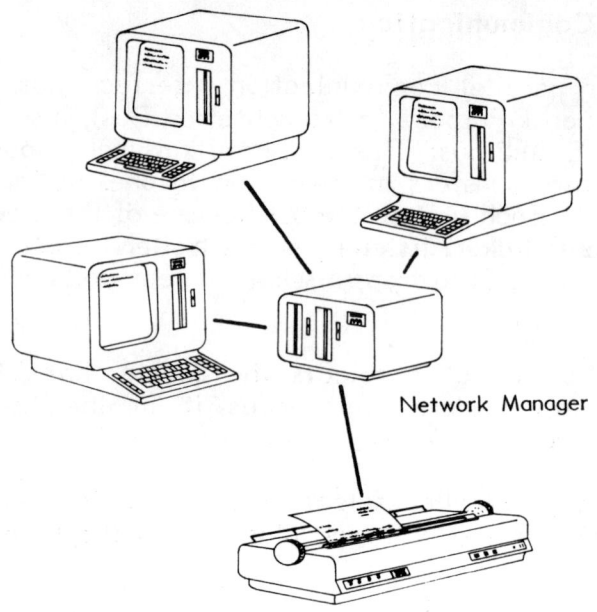

Figure 6-4   A Star Network Configuration. All devices are connected only to the network manager.

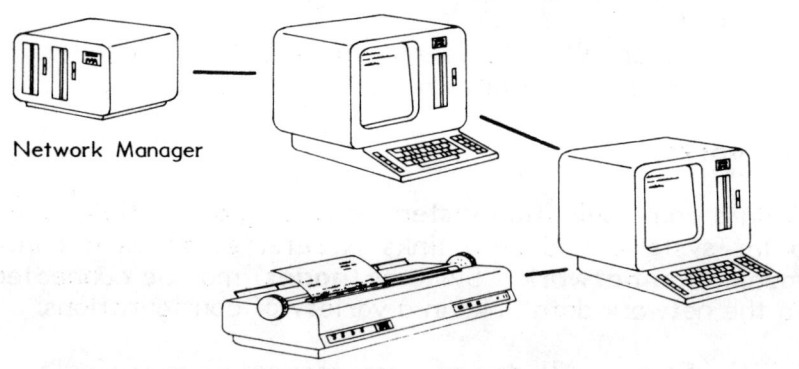

Figure 6-5   A Daisy Chain Network Configuration. Each device is connected to two other devices.

2) **Daisy Chain** - Devices are connected together in a chain (Figure 6-5). The first device in the chain is the network master. Communication from the network master to any other device in the chain must pass through all devices between them.

3) **Ring** - All devices are attached to the network master in a loop (Figure 6-6). Messages from the network master must pass through each prior device in the loop before reaching the assigned destination.

4) **Multidrop** - All nodes are connected to a single communication cable (Figure 6-7). Each node receives all messages sent along the cable. Each node has a unique bus address and ignores messages not coded with the correct address. Any node may communicate with any other node on the data link.

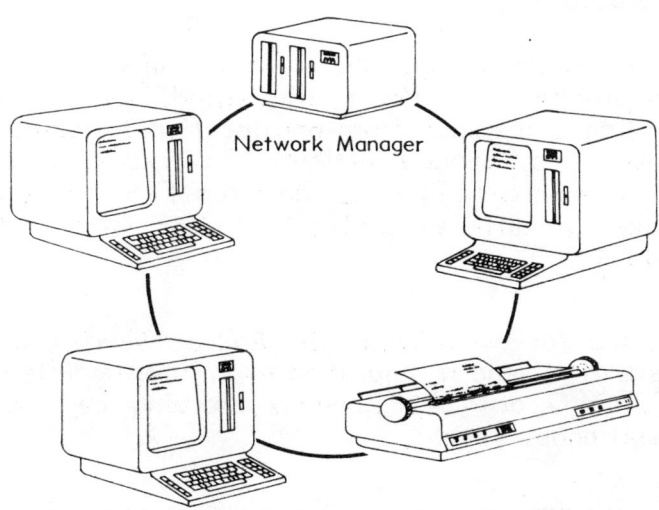

Figure 6-6   A Ring or Loop Network Configuration. Each device is connected to two other devices and the data link begins and ends with the network manager.

System Control and Communication

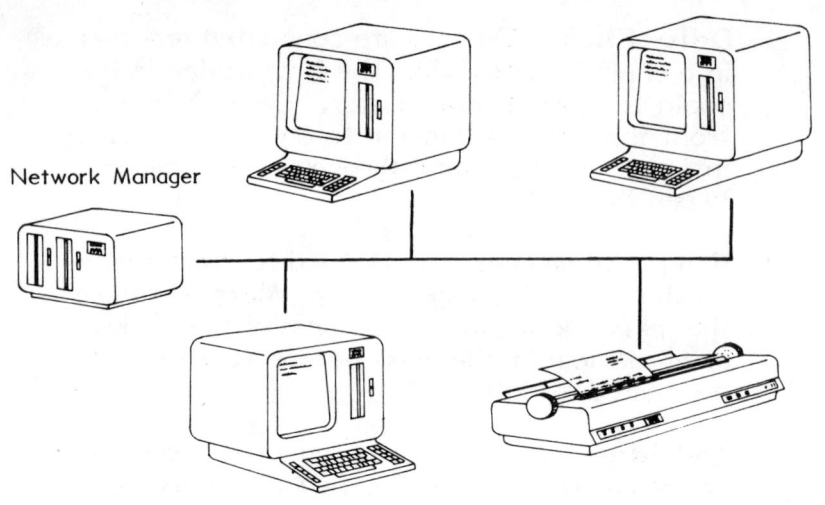

Figure 6-7 A Multidrop Network Configuration. Each device is connected independently to the data link.

Packet Switching

Very large communication networks are often composed of many smaller networks as illustrated in Figure 6-8. Transmitting a message from one location to another in this network may be very difficult. For example, in this network, transmission of a message from R to H may take place over two different paths: R-P-K-F-G-H or R-P-A-F-G-H.

One method for establishing the link between R and H requires that R send a request to each intermediate node (P, K, F, and G, or P, A, F, and G) reserving the data link to the next node.

Once all required data links have been granted, R begins transmitting messages. This method (**line switching**) is similar to the use of public telephone lines. This method of communication has one major disadvantage. Once

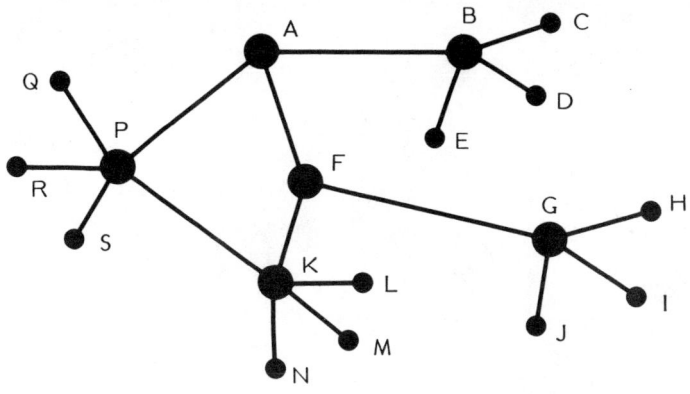

Figure 6-8   A Large Communication Network.

R has reserved a connection (e.g., F to G) no other device can use the same connection until R releases it (even though R uses only a portion of the data link bandwidth).

Packet switching implementations solve this cost sensitive bandwidth utilization problem by dividing all messages into fixed size information packets. To transmit a message, the source node formats one or more packets and forwards the packets to the nearest node on the communication link (R transmits to P in this example). Whenever a node receives a packet of information that is not addressed to it, the node temporarily stores and subsequently retransmits the packet over the best available data path. This technique is known as a **store-and-foward** strategy. In this example, P would forward packets to either K or A depending on data link utilization and availability. All message packets ultimately reach their destination and are reassembled into the original message. It is interesting to note that portions of large messages may be transmitted simultaneously to the destination node over separate data links. For example, packets can be transmitted from P to F along two links simultaneously (P-A-F and P-K-F).

System Control and Communication

Chapter 7

Serial, Parallel, and Distributed Processing

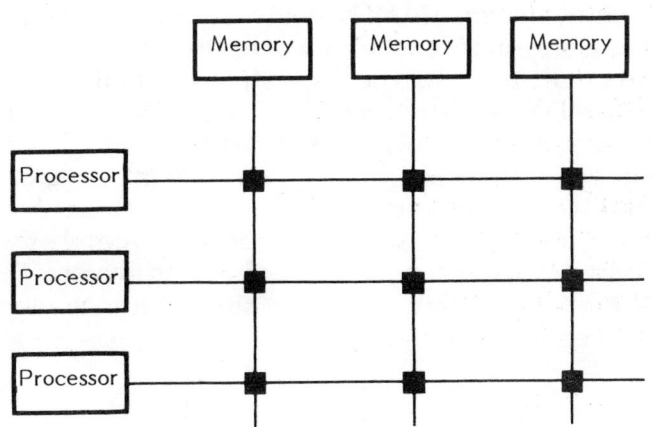

Most processors in use today operate in a **serial** (sequential) manner, executing one instruction at a time and performing one memory or I/O access at a time. By combining multiple ALUs within a processor or by combining multiple processors within a system, **parallel** (simultaneous) processing is possible. Parallel processing greatly enhances system throughput. When every processor in a parallel configuration contains its own memory and I/O, the system is termed **distributed**. A distributed system allows complex functions to be divided into smaller independent activities. Each processor in a distributed system functions independently, coordinating operations by means of a data link or bus.

Systems are often categorized in terms of **instruction streams** and **data streams.** An instruction stream is a single sequential flow of instructions (e.g., a task or process) executed by a processor. A data stream is a single flow of data elements into and out of a processor. Most conventional architectures are classed as single instruction stream, single data stream **(SISD)** units. Parallel ALU units that operate on more than one data element simultaneously under control of a single instruction (e.g., array processors) are single instruction stream, multiple data stream **(SIMD)** devices. Independent parallel processors that execute multiple tasks simultaneously are multiple instruction stream, multiple data stream **(MIMD)** architectures. Finally, when a single data item is simultaneously processed by several instructions, the term multiple instruction stream, single data stream **(MISD)** is applied. MISD architectures are not common; graphics processors that recognize features within a picture by simultaneously performing several rotations and matching operations on a single picture element are considered MISD units.

Serial Processing

Serial precessors execute instructions one at a time. Not only are the instructions fetched and executed in a serial manner, but a single instruction cycle is normally broken down into a set of subcycles (states). During each state, a set of well-defined processor functions are performed (Figure 7-1).

State Number	
1	Output instruction address
2	Activate memory read signal
3	Wait
4	Latch instruction
5	Compute effective address
6	Output effective address
7	Activate memory read signal
8	Wait
9	Add data to accumulator
10	Test interrupt request signal

Figure 7-1   A Ten State Instruction Cycle for an ADD Instruction.

Serial processors are often programmed to give users the illusion of parallel processing. A multiprogramming operating system with a clock interrupt periodically allows each task to use the processor for a short period of time. When one task is waiting for a user input or for an I/O transfer, the processor is free to execute other tasks. To a user of the system, this processor multiplexing generates the appearance of a large number of slightly slower processors executing in parallel.

Pipelines

Serial processing throughput may be enhanced by **pipelining**. A pipeline operates in the same manner as an assembly line where a complex operation is decomposed into a sequential set of n single operations. When the first item enters the assembly line (pipe), all assembly stations are idle. One clock cycle later, after the first operation is complete, the item moves to the second station and a new item simultaneously enters the first station. The two assembly operations proceed simultaneously. After n clock cycles, the first completed unit is delivered from the end of the assembly line. Each clock cycle thereafter, another completed unit is delivered and a new item enters the line.

Pipelines are utilized when a complex function must be performed sequentially on a large number of data elements (e.g., floating point vector addition). If the function can be decomposed into a set of independent operations, a pipeline can be designed. Pipelined units with n independent operations approach n times the speed of a non-pipelined processor as illustrated in Figure 7-2.

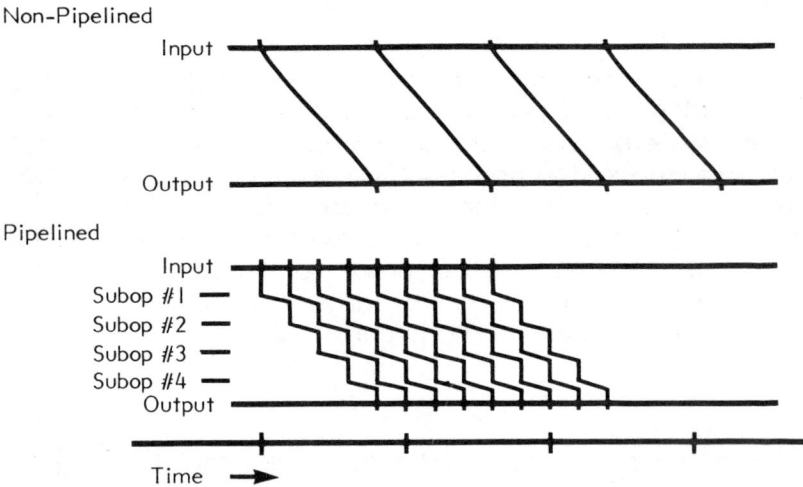

Figure 7-2 A Time Line Comparison of Pipelining versus Normal Processing. The non-pipelined operations require four time periods. For pipelining, each operation is divided into four suboperations that need one time period apiece. Nine pipelined operations can be performed in the same amount of time as three non-pipelined operations.

Pipelines may be used to process instructions as well as data. One common technique to increase performance overlaps the instruction fetch and execute cycle. While the processor is busy performing computations on data internally, the next instruction is fetched from the bus. A technique called **prefetching** can fetch a large number of instructions (limited only by the maximum processor queue size). Whenever the processor is ready to fetch an instruction, the instruction is normally waiting in the queue. Instructions are fetched whenever the bus is idle. If a program control instruction causes the program counter to be modified, the queue is flushed and the prefetching operation starts again. Extensive prefetching can easily reach a point of "diminishing returns" when a program contains many branch instructions. If the instruction queue is significantly longer than the average execution distance between program branches, the processor will routinely prefetch too many instructions, thereby wasting valuable memory bandwidth.

If desired, prefetching techniques can be extended to cover conditional and unconditional data transfers. By installing additional queues, instructions may be prefetched from all possible branch destinations. When the branch actually occurs, instructions are taken from the queue representing the correct branch destination; all other queues are flushed.

Parallel Processors

Parallel processors execute multiple instructions or operate on multiple data elements simultaneously. The simplest conceptual form of parallel processing hardware incorporates multiple ALUs within a single processor. Processors with multiple ALUs can peform operations on many data elements at the same time. Since this form of processing allows efficient vector and array operations, computer designs that include processors with multiple ALUs are known as **array processors.** The term array processor is often used incorrectly to describe a separate serial processing unit (usually pipelined) dedicated to floating point array manipulations. When the term array processor is used in this context, the term "vector processor" is used to describe processors with multiple ALUs.

The largest problem encountered with a multiple ALU architecture is memory bandwidth. Multiple high-speed ALUs require an exceptionally wide data bus coupled with the ability to simultaneously access independent memory banks. A second problem is control coordination among various ALUs (especially for non-array calculations). In order to maximize processor performance, the processor control unit must attempt to keep all ALUs busy and avoid conflicts. Conflicts between ALUs easily occur when the processor is executing sequential code and attempting as much parallel calculation as possible. New operations often require the results of previous operations. If a previous operation has not yet been completed, the new operation cannot be started on a free ALU. Instead the processor must idle until the previous calculation is complete.

Coprocessors

The concept of a **coprocessor, extended processing unit (EPU),** or **slave processor** is analogous to a system of multiple ALUs and is a popular method of extending microprocessor instruction sets and processing power. A coprocessor is a processing unit designed to reside on a microprocessor bus and communicate control information to the master system processor by means of a few dedicated signal lines.

When, in the course of executing instructions, the master processor decodes a special coprocessor instruction prefix or the master processor decodes an instruction that is not implemented in its instruction set, the processor determines if the correct coprocessor is attached to the bus. If the coprocessor is available, the master processor permits the coprocessor to execute the instruction. If the coprocessor is not attached to the processor bus, the master processor forces an exception condition (Chapter 11) and a software module performs the same functions as does the coprocessor (at a much slower rate).

When a coprocessor is executing an instruction, the coprocessor may take complete control of the bus to access data or the master processor may perform the actual addressing functions. Once the coprocessor begins execution the master processor may be permitted to continue executing until it either decodes another instruction requiring the busy coprocessor or until a *wait for completion* instruction is encountered (signaling that the coprocessor computation is needed before the next instruction is executed).

Coprocessors are typically designed for extended arithmetic (e.g., floating point and trigonometric functions), data base manipulation, and list management.

Multiprocessing

Multiprocessing is a parallel processing technique in which a set of independent processors sequentially execute instructions for different tasks. Each processor has identical access to system memory. The system may utilize a single memory bus that is shared by all processors or multiple busses (one for each processor) may be used as illustrated in Figure 7-3. Multiprocessing systems may be tightly or loosely coupled. **Tightly coupled** systems implement an execution philosophy known as **load sharing**. A load sharing system utilizes a single operating system and task scheduling algorithm that attempts to share the system computational load equally among all processors within the system.

When a processor becomes idle in a load sharing system (e.g., when the current task has completed execution or is waiting for an event), the operating system selects another task that is ready to execute and starts the task executing on the idle processor. A single task, under this strategy,

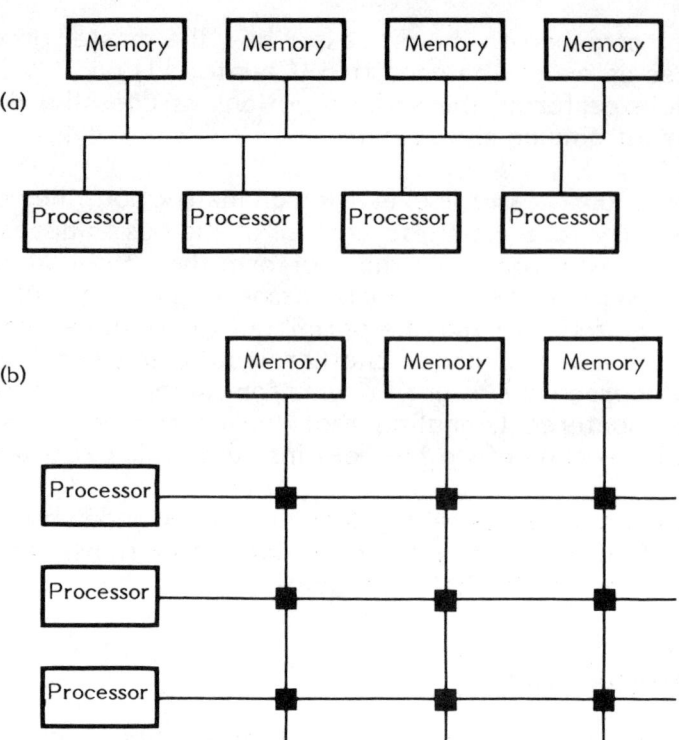

Figure 7-3   Multiprocessing Configurations: (a) a single high-speed bus and (b) crossbar switches (multiple independent memory access busses).

may begin executing on one processor, stop executing while it waits for input, and then resume execution on a different processor. Since all processors are identical, the task software can detect no difference from one processor to another. Load sharing permits maximum utilization of the processing capacity of a multiprocessing system.

A **loosely coupled** system typically executes as two computer systems. The only interaction within a loosely coupled system is a resource manager that permits one of the multiple processors to gain exclusive use of a resource (e.g., an I/O device) for a specified operation. Loosely coupled systems often partition memory so that each processor does not interfere with the others.

I/O Processors

A common form of multiprocessing employs the use of two processors: the general purpose system processor and an **I/O processor** or **I/O channel**. An I/O processor is a special purpose processor that is dedicated to, and optimized for, input and output functions such as block data transfers, error detection, and interrupt service. I/O processors have been used for many years in system designs. I/O functions and general processing functions are different enough so that, in most cases, both processors operate independently and simultaneously. I/O processors are discussed in more detail in Chapter 9.

Content-Addressable Processors

A **content-addressable** processor may be thought of as the ultimate parallel processing architecture. Every memory word in a content-addressable processor is in fact a miniature ALU. Each memory word ALU must be capable of: comparing broadcast data against the contents of one or more fields within the memory word and writing data to selected fields whenever a comparison match occurs. All memory words in which a match occurs are **responders.**

The major benefit offered by content-addressable parallel processors is the ability to eliminate time consuming loops of instructions by performing equivalent computations in a fixed number of machine instructions. With a serial processor, the execution time of an algorithm is directly proportional to the number of items in an array. With a content-addressable processor, the execution time of the same algorithm is fixed, independent of the number of items in the array. For example, to search an employment file for employees who earn $30,000 per year and have been employed for 5 years just two instructions are required regardless of the number of employees in the file. The first instruction broadcasts the representation of 30,000 and instructs the memory to compare this data with its SALARY field. All matches will set the TAG bit within the responders. The second instruction broadcasts the number

5 and instructs the memory to compare against the EMPYR field when the TAG field is set. All responders (after this instruction) fulfill the two initial conditions.

Obviously many information processing problems (especially data base management functions) require exactly this matching capability! Content-addressable memories, however, are still considerably larger and more expensive than ordinary random access memories used today in most computer systems.

A content-addressable processor consists of a control unit, a program memory, and a content-addressable (associative memory) as shown in Figure 7-4. The program memory architecture is normally identical to the program memory in other computer systems; instructions are executed sequentially with conditional and unconditional branches. Programs are stored in a random access memory. Programs can not easily be stored in a content-addressable memory since program control is basically sequential and well-structured and a content-addressable memory can not be addressed sequentially.

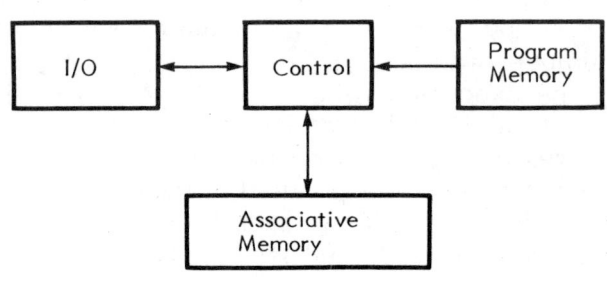

Figure 7-4   Content-Addressable Processor Configuration.

The control unit within a content addressable processor directs program execution, content-addressable memory operations, and I/O. An associative word in memory consists of data fields and tags (Figure 7-5). For matching and writing operations, data fields are normally delineated by means of memory masks. Associative memory words are often very wide (64-256 bits).

One important feature that is included in some content-addressable processor designs is the notion of direction between words in the content-addressable memory. The concept of direction permits one memory cell to pass the contents of a tag field on to the next memory word in any of four directions (up, down, left, or right). This capability is extremely useful in operations such as text string searches. For example, to search for the word "YES" in a string, three instructions are executed. The first instructon broadcasts the letter "Y" to the content-addressable memory specifying that all matches pass the TAG to the memory word on the right. The second instruction broadcasts the letter "E" and requires a match plus a set TAG. The TAG is again passed to the right. The final instruction broadcasts the letter "S", again requiring a match and a set TAG. All responders at this point indicate positions of the "YES" substring in the original string.

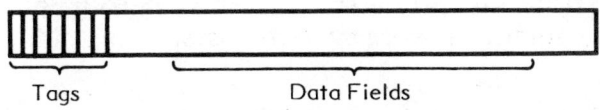

Figure 7-5 A Word of Associative Memory Consists of Tags (to indicate matches and permit logic operations) and Multiple Data Fields. Associative memory words are often very wide (up to 256 bits).

Serial, Parallel, and Distributed Processing

Distributed Processing

The complexity of controlling systems with multiple processors grows rapidly as the number of processors increases. In addition, multiprocessor systems typically require extremely high memory bandwidths and wide data paths. **Distributed processing** lowers system complexity by decomposing system functions into small stand-alone tasks that can be executed on individual microprocessor systems. The low cost of microprocessor hardware, the small size of microcomputer systems, and the relative ease of writing dedicated software is constantly accelerating this trend toward **distributed intelligence.**

The key to distributed processing system development is a reliable high-speed communication network as described in Chapter 6. This communication network permits each microprocessor system to function independently, yet transfer information and coordinate actions with other independent processors. Each network node (system) is treated as a black box, performing its functions with its own intelligence and resources.

Distributed processing can achieve significant cost savings over custom designed systems. Each distributed controller unit is often a standard preprogrammed single-chip microcomputer. Total software development costs are distributed over a very high sales volume. Because of the network's communications capabilities, expensive devices such as printers and disk drives can be shared among multiple distributed processors. This **resource sharing** capability further lowers system costs.

An interesting example of distributed processing is found in the "office of the future," an office environment in which most office machines are intelligent components of a communications network. This communications network supports devices such as:

1) Secretarial Terminal - A typewriter or keyboard/display unit that contains a one or two

page internal text buffer. This unit can send information to a data base unit for filing and/or retrieval, it can print memos or draft copies locally, and it can transmit finished letters electronically to other locations.

2) Printer/Copier - Receives text (memos, reports) electronically from other terminals in the network and produces hard copy.

3) Word Processing System - Edits reports, manuals, and other large documents. These documents may be archived locally, sent to the data base (to be shared by other systems), or sent to a printer for hard copy. Documents could also be transmitted over telephone lines to a remote photocomposition facility.

4) Management Information Terminal - This unit permits an employee to view accounting and forecasting data (tabular and graphic displays). The terminal requests raw data from the data base and reformats the data into graphical representations. Software in the terminal produces six-month forecasts and required stocking levels. These terminals also maintain tickler files and "things to do today" lists for employees.

5) Data Base - This unit stores documents, customer files, order backlogs, inventory and shipping information, and other pertinent office data. Other devices within the system may receive data/text from the data base or send data to it for storage.

6) Facsimile/Modem - Accepts pages of text or graphics and transmits this information over telephone lines to a receiving unit.

7) Order Entry Terminal - Accesses the data base and updates customer orders, backlogs, etc.

8) Production Terminal - Used for inventory control and parts forecasting. Provides access to parts lists, kit build schedules, and ordering specifications.

9) Test Equipment - Monitors parts testing and inventory rework. This information is transmitted to the data base and is used to compute mean time between failures (MTBF) and to isolate manufacturing problems as they arise.

10) Data Processing Unit - Accesses the data base and produces standard business reports. It is also used in conjunction with a management information terminal for scientific and engineering calculations.

Distributed processing is also found in many other applications areas in addition to the office. Some examples are:

1) Process Control - Individual process controllers are independently functioning units. A set of process optimization goals is sent to each controller from a central computer system. If the central computer system fails, the individual controllers can keep the process running smoothly and without danger.

2) Transportation - Intersections or railroad interlockings are controlled by distributed processing units. A central control algorithm performs route minimization for optimized fuel economy. If the central control computer fails, the distributed units can operate the intersections or interlockings under manual or automatic control.

3) Home - Distributed processors can control the furnace, oven, lawn sprinklers, lighting, and telephone dialing under the direction of a low-cost central control unit. The complete system is affordable only if each unit is mass-produced.

Security and Reliability

Parallel processing techniques are often used to build highly reliable systems with little or no down-time due to system failures. Architectural designs that allow a system to continue operating in the face of single or multiple component failures are termed **fault tolerant.** Performance degradation in a fault tolerant system (after a component failure) is known as **graceful degradation.**

Three basic methods are commonly used to implement fault tolerant systems. The simplest method involves the use of a dual processor configuration. One system is designated the primary processor and the other system is the backup. Periodically, the primary processor transmits a data base dump of critical information (called a **checkpoint**) to the backup processor. If the primary processor fails to transmit this information, system control automatically passes to the backup processor. The backup processor gains control of all system resources and begins execution with the data saved at the last checkpoint. After the primary processor has been repaired, system control is passed back to the primary processor under operator command. While the primary processor is operating, the backup processor is often used for other jobs such as program editing, simulation, and training in order not to waste processing resources.

A second technique used in critical process control and aerospace applications involves three or more processors and a reliability technique known as **voting.** All processors in a voting system operate on the same inputs. Before control signals are issued, commands from all processors are compared. If a single processor is in disagreement, an alarm signal is generated and the dissenting processor is outvoted.

The third and most advanced method of reliable multiprocessor architecture permits processors to be added to, or deleted from, the system at any time while the system is operating. All processors in this architecture are identical, containing a small amount of private memory. In addition, shared memory modules and I/O interfaces are included in the system. All components of the system are interconnected by a set of bus couplers. All essential system information is replicated in two or more independent modules. Failing modules can be automatically uncoupled from the remainder of the system to preserve integrity. In this architecture, individual component failures may degrade system performance but individual failures cannot cause catastrophic system failures.

Chapter 8

Memory and Resource Access and Protection

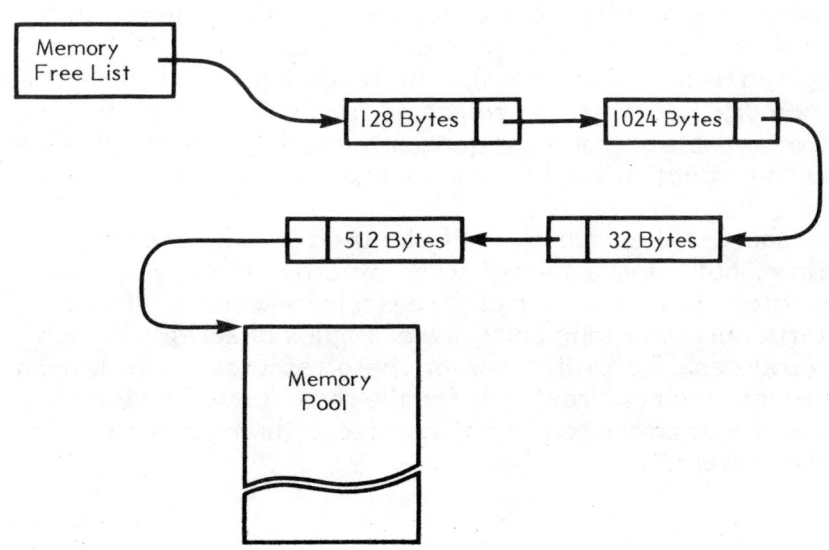

Computer system assets such as primary and secondary memory space, peripheral devices, and processors are all system **resources**. System resources are used by tasks to process and store information, send/receive messages, and perform data input and output. Economic and physical constraints on the quantity of resources available within a system make it imperative that the system share resources among a large number of contending software tasks.

Resources must be **allocated** to a task before the resources may be used. **Protection** mechanisms are designed to ensure that a task can only access resources that are allocated for its use.

Consumable and Reusable Resources

System resources are divided into two classes: **consumable resources** and **serially reusable resources**. A consumable resource is produced by one task within the computer system (the **producer**) and consumed by another task (the **consumer**). For example, messages are placed into a memory segment by the producer (the memory segment is allocated to the producing task by the system). The message is sent to another task where it is consumed (read and acted on). The receiving task discards the memory segment by releasing it back to the system. Consumable resources generally have a short lifetime with respect to the lifetime of tasks within the system.

Resources that can normally be used by only one task at a time, but can be reused later by other tasks, are appropriately known as serially reusable resources. Printers, terminals, and tape units are examples of serially reusable resources. To utilize one of these resources, a task must request the resource, wait for the resource to be allocated, use the resource, and finally, release the resource back to the system.

Resource Management

Serially reusable resources are normally controlled by a single resource manager (possibly one for each resource type). The resource manager fields resource requests and allocates resources to tasks on a first-come first-served or priority basis. Two resource allocation strategies are normally used. The first strategy actually passes complete and exclusive resource control to the requesting task. The resource is no longer free for use by other tasks until the original task releases the resource. The system maintains tables of current resource allocation at all times. This type of allocation strategy is often employed to allocate user terminals within a multiuser programming environment. From the time a user enters the system, his terminal is under exclusive control of a single user task.

The second allocation strategy focuses on providing resource services to tasks rather than providing actual physical resources. In this method, a task requests service (e.g., printing) from the system. The system then controls and allocates the use of resources as appropriate without ever relinquishing direct resource control to the requesting tasks.

Consumable resources utilize memory segments to contain the information used by a task or passed from task to task. The system is responsible for all segment accesses as discussed in Chapter 5. All segments are created by the system in response to task requests. Each segment can grow and contract under direct control of the requesting task.

Memory Management

In systems where paging is not implemented, or the number of segments permitted within a task is limited, memory allocation takes place from reserved memory **pools**. The system allocates all segments from a single free pool of primary storage. Tasks often request segments and subdivide these segments into a number of pools. Messages and I/O buffers may be allocated from multiple pools within the same segment.

Initially, a pool begins as a contiguous logical memory area. The memory manager allocates memory to a task by removing a block of the required size from the pool and informing the requesting task of its position. Some systems add a message header to the allocated memory and actually send the block as a message to the requesting task that is then free to use the memory as needed.

As memory blocks are returned to the memory manager, a list of free blocks is built (Figure 8-1). Additional memory requests cause the memory manager to first examine the list to determine if one of the returned blocks satisfies the request before removing memory from the remaining pool. Two strategies can be used to allocate the requested memory from available blocks. The simplest is known as the **first fit** algorithm, where the first block large enough to satisfy the request is used for allocation. The second method, the **best fit** algorithm, finds the available memory block that is closest in size to the requested block. Referring to Figure 8-1, a request for 30 bytes would be allocated from the 128 byte area using the first fit method and from the 32 byte area with the best fit method. Intuitively, the best fit algorithm seems superior since it wastes the least amount of memory during allocation (although it is the slower of the two methods). However, simulations have determined that the first fit strategy is simpler and leads to less memory fragmentation.

Often, the memory manager is designed to concatenate two memory blocks if a returned block is logically adjacent to a block already in the free list. This larger block usually provides more allocation flexibility than two small blocks. If blocks are not automatically joined when they are returned, large memory blocks tend to be continuously broken into smaller pieces. Breaking up large memory blocks can lead to a condition known as **fragmentation** where leftover sections of memory are too small to fill an allocation request. When fragmentation occurs, and a request is made for a contiguous block larger than those on the list, the memory manager must perform **garbage collection** on the free list. Garbage collection is a time-

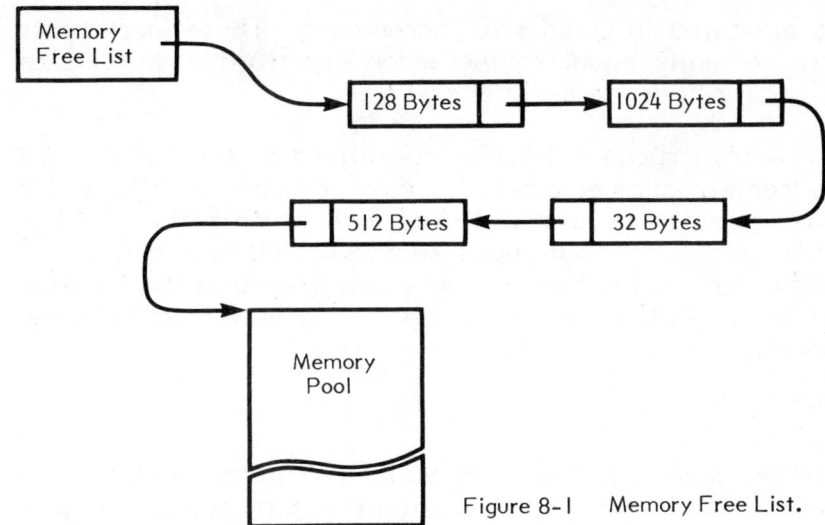

Figure 8-1 Memory Free List.

consuming function where the free list is scanned from beginning to end and all contiguous blocks are concatenated. If this operation yields a block large enough to satisfy the request, the block is allocated to the requester. If a large enough block is still not available, but the total free memory space (all free blocks added together) is large enough to satisfy the request, allocated blocks may be moved in the memory space to close up small blocks of scattered free space.

Memory management problems on free memory pools are considerably eased if all buffers or messages allocated from a pool are the same size. In this case, the system treats the pool as a single fixed list of buffers, and fragmentation (and the resulting garbage collection) will never occur.

File Allocation

File allocation (secondary storage allocation) is normally treated in the same manner as is primary storage allocation with the additional constraint that storage space is allocated in fixed size increments. These increments are normally equal to the secondary storage sector size (Chapter 9) or the system page size.

Because garbage collection operations on a large disk are extremely cumbersome, the most flexible technique for file allocation uses a linked list organization (rather than requiring contiguous sectors). With a linked list organization, the file directory entry contains the location of the file's first sector, and each file sector contains the location of the next sector in the file.

Rather than requiring each sector link to physically reside in the file sector, many systems create pointer sectors (similar to page tables for paged segments) for each file. Each pointer sector contains the locations for a fixed number of sectors within the file. The number of pointer sectors needed for a file is determined from the file size by a simple ratio as demonstrated in Figure 8-2.

Managing a free list (of sectors) across the entire disk surface may cause excessive seek and latency delays as sectors are allocated and freed. To enhance secondary storage management performance, many systems use a free space allocation technique known as a **bit map**. A bit in the bit map is set aside for each sector on the disk; a set bit indicates that the corresponding sector is allocated, while a cleared bit indicates that the corresponding sector is free. The first bit in the bit map corresponds to the first sector on the disk, and the last bit in the map corresponds to the last sector on the disk. The bit map is small in size since only one bit is used to represent a complete sector. The bit map is physically placed close to the volume directory so disk head movement is minimized. Allocation and freeing of sectors is accomplished by simply altering the bit map. No other sectors need be read, written, or rewritten.

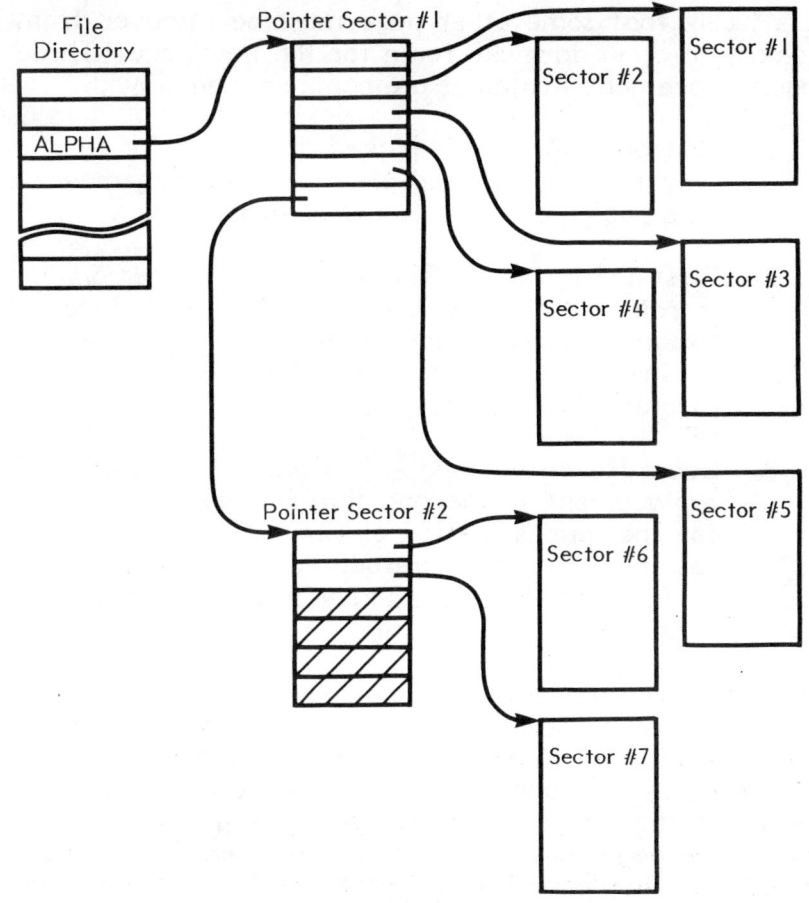

Figure 8-2 File Storage with Pointer Sectors. The illustrated file contains seven sectors. If each pointer sector contains n pointers, the number of pointer sectors required for a file is m/n, where m is the file size in sectors. In this example, two pointer sectors are required.

Management with Paging

Paging, if implemented, permits unused portions of a segment to be stored on a secondary storage device (such as a disk drive) until that portion of the segment is accessed. When a page must be moved into memory from secondary storage (in order to service a page fault),

Memory and Resource Access and Protection

it is likely that some other page must be removed from memory in order to make room for the new page. Three page replacement strategies are commonly employed:

1) Random - A page is picked at random for removal. The removed page, on occasion, may be a page required to continue execution.

2) First-In First-Out - The oldest page in memory is selected for replacement. This technique assumes that the least likely page to be used in the future is the page that has been in memory the longest.

3) Least Recently Used - The page selected for replacement is the one that has been unused for the longest period of time. This strategy assumes pages that are unused for long periods of time are the least likely to be used in the future.

To increase system efficiency, pages to be replaced need not be copied to secondary storage if these pages have not been altered. Program segment pages often fall into this category. If a page has not been altered, its secondary storage image is identical to its memory image, and a new page may simply be copied over the memory image. To implement this replacement algorithm, each page table entry contains a flag (called the **dirty bit**) that is set whenever the page is written. If the dirty bit is set, the memory image of the page has been altered and may no longer agree with its secondary storage image.

Thrashing

Paging systems require considerable system overhead to service page faults. If a large number of programs are executing (as in a large time sharing environment), a point can be reached where page faults occur so often that system efficiency is drastically degraded. This state is known as **thrashing,** as the system is literally flailing away moving pages to and from secondary storage. This condition can become so extreme that system overhead approaches 100% of total system availability and no useful work is accomplished. An example of what happens to the system during thrashing is illustrated by the following scenario. As a task executes, it needs a new page moved into memory. The system finds a page (in memory) to replace and begins the I/O operation to load the new page. While the I/O operation is functioning, the system attempts to execute another task. This task begins executing, but it references the page that is currently being replaced. Another page fault occurs, the system selects another task for execution, and the same scenario repeats. In this scenario, the system keeps replacing pages that are needed by other tasks to run, so no task can successfully execute.

The problem with most page replacement algorithms is that they can cause paging interactions between two independent tasks as shown above, where each task's required pages keep getting replaced (in order to start other tasks executing). Every task needs a set of pages in memory to run for a given period of time. This set of pages is called the **working set.** The size of this set may be approximated by periodically measuring the number of pages used by a task and assuming that the size of the working set will vary slowly with respect to time. This working set is highly dependent on overall task structure and I/O. It cannot easily be predicted in advance.

The working set concept can be used to eliminate thrashing if a task is loaded for execution only when the system has determined that there are sufficient free pages in memory to contain the task working set without disrupting other tasks. The page replacement strategy for this working set policy first removes pages from memory belonging to the task that is currently page faulted to eliminate task interactions.

Protection

All software executing within a computer system is vulnerable to errors and malfunctions of the system. These malfunctions may be hardware errors (e.g., memory errors) or software errors (e.g., subscript range errors). The protection features designed into a computer system directly impact the reliability and security of software running on the system. Systems with good protection features detect and isolate errors when they occur, before they can corrupt system-wide data structures and lead to total system failure. System protection is closely allied with the topic of error detection. Hardware and software error detection and hardware error correction is discussed in Chapter 11.

Software malfunctions may be accidental or malicious. In either case, the system should protect system software and user software modules as well as I/O devices and other system resources from unauthorized access or modification. Implementation of protection functions within a computer system without hardware support for **access right** qualification is a tedious software job. Software protection functions translate into phenomenally high system overhead. Many currently manufactured systems (especially microprocessor systems) contain no hardware protection support. Software on these systems cannot be easily protected. Software design for these systems must assume a **friendly environment,** that is, an environment in which both hardware and software has been extensively tested. No provisions can be made to isolate software or hardware failures, gracefully degrade system performance, or protect tasks from either hardware or software malfunctions.

Generally, protection features can be divided into three closely related areas. First, system software such as the operating system, system management tables, link segments, and page tables must be protected against modification by unauthorized tasks. System software must also be protected against internal errors, at least to the extent of detecting errors when they occur (Chapter 11). System software security is the most important aspect of system protection since violations of system data integrity quickly cause the entire system to cease functioning.

The second area of protection involves a task's vulnerability to the errors and malfunctions of other tasks. The system must protect tasks against unauthorized access from other tasks within the system as well as from internal software errors. Finally, system resources must be protected from unauthorized use. System resources are I/O devices, disk files, and memory buffer areas.

Protection mechanisms may be thought of as defending all system **objects** (Chapter 4) against unauthorized access. Attempted infringements of protection mechanisms are referred to as **protection violations.**

Object Protection

Protection mechanisms must protect system objects against inherent object misuse. These mechanisms perform checks to ensure that:

1) All program accesses reference valid system objects.

2) Object addresses are within the valid address space of the referenced object.

3) The specified type of object access is valid for the defined object.

Object protection should always be performed on the basis of the object's logical address. Logical protection mechanisms associate protection information with the segment descriptor for an object. Generally, a segment length and an access code are included in the segment descriptor. The segment length is used to verify that a specified logical address exists within the segment. The access code specifies the type of object accesses that are permitted.

Typical object independent access codes permit:

1) No Access

2) Read Only Access

3) Read/Write Access

4) Execute Only Access

In addition, object dependent access codes may be specified to limit the types of valid operations that may be performed on an object. For example:

1) For a stack object, the valid operations are PUSH, POP, EXCHANGE, and DUPLICATE.

2) For a data object or file, the valid operations are READ, WRITE, APPEND, and RENAME.

3) For an I/O object, the valid operations are INPUT, OUTPUT, STATUS, and CONTROL.

Some systems implement object protection on a physical memory basis. All segments and/or page frames in physical memory have an access code. Segments or portions of segments for many different tasks may coexist in physical memory at any given time. To preserve integrity when a task is suspended from execution, the system software must change the access codes for all memory page frames belonging to the suspended task to "No Access" and reenable correct accesses for the segments belonging to the next executing task. A method intended to avoid this system overhead uses software keys that must be presented to gain access to a page frame. Page frame protection by means of software keys is unsatisfactory unless the key is large enough to prevent accidental presentation of a valid key (by an unauthorized task) for a protected page frame.

Access Path Protection

In addition to protecting an object from invalid access, protection mechanisms may also be placed on the **access path** of an object. Access path protection allows the system to provide different levels of protection for an object depending on the circumstances under which the object is referenced. A shared data segment within a single task offers a good example of the difference between access path and object protection mechanisms. With object protection only, all program segments would be forced to have the same access restrictions. It would be impossible to permit Write access to the object from one segment while restricting all other segments to Read Only access.

Privileged Instructions

All protection mechanisms depend heavily on the concept of **privileged instructions.** A privileged instruction is a processor instruction that should only be executed by system software because of its potential for system damage. For example, the following instructions are normally classified as privileged:

1) Input and Output Instructions

2) Interrupt Control Instructions

3) Halt Instruction

4) Instructions that Load, Store, or Modify Segment or Page Registers

5) Instructions that Modify Access Codes

6) Unused Operation Codes

To utilize privileged instructions, processor operation is normally divided into two modes: **user mode** and **privileged (system) mode.** In practice, no user task is permitted to operate in the system mode. The operating system is the only software that is permitted to utilize privileged instructions.

In some architectures, the ability to execute privileged instructions is tied to the logical memory address. These designs divide the logical address space into system and user areas. When executing in the system area, all privileged instructions may be executed.

Levels of Protection

Control of the access paths to objects is considerably more difficult than simple object-oriented protection. One method of specifying intersegment access rights defines an access matrix for each task. The access matrix contains rows and columns for each segment within the process. The access right for a reference from segment Y to segment X is found in row X and column Y of the access matrix. This protection mechanism is difficult to manage because of its potentially large size. A more easily implemented scheme envisions the access protection problem as a set of protection levels. Protection levels are implemented in a ring structure (Figure 8-3). The innermost rings contain the most trusted software — the operating system kernel, the system executive, and the applications supervisor. Proceeding from the inner to the outer layers, software is less trusted and more protection is installed. Any level can access within its own level or access an outer level without restriction. Entry to inner level segments can only occur through well-defined entry points called **gates.** The access to an inner level is controlled by the operating system by means of **service calls** or **programmed operators.**

Access in this manner does pose some problems, however. One problem arises because the operating system functions can access segments that the calling task cannot access. For example, a calling task could pass an invalid address to a system service function. The system service, executing in a more trusted protection level, might be permitted

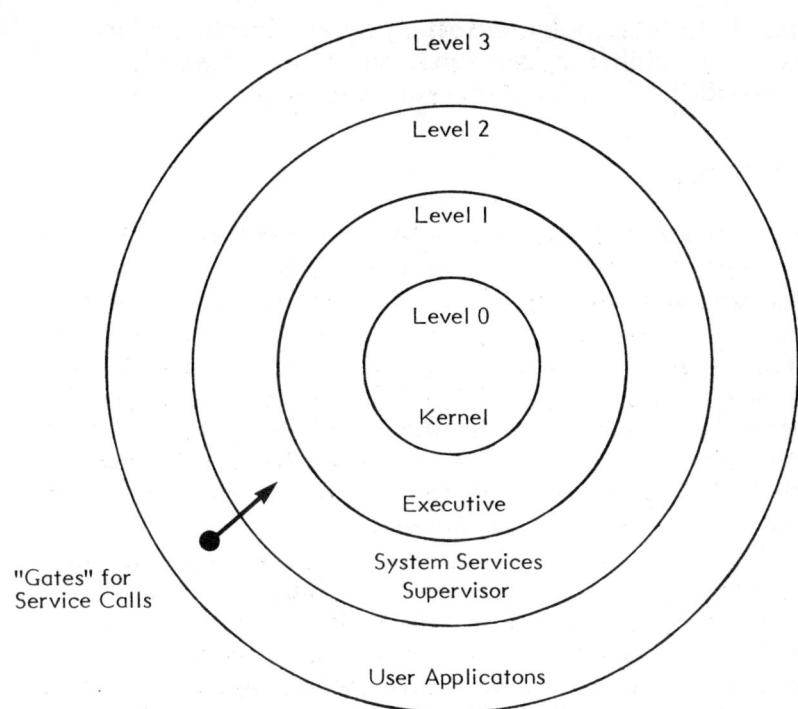

Figure 8-3 Rings (Levels) of Protection. Access from an outer level to an inner level takes place only through well-defined "gates" by means of system service calls.

to access the invalid address and damage another task. To avoid unauthorized accesses, special software or hardware functions must be invoked to determine if the addresses passed to the system service functions are valid for the calling segment. In addition, all parameters must be physically copied into the system's data area. If the parameters are not copied, another task (sharing the calling task's data area) could subsequently change the parameters after they had been validated by the system.

Actual implementation of this ring protection structure is normally restricted to a small number of rings (4 or 8). The processor status word can then contain the current execution ring level. In this implementation, determination of access rights is a straightforward function of task execution ring number and the level of the referenced segment.

Capabilities

The ring structure for access rights assumes that the innermost levels of software are free from errors. This assumption is only partially true. Many systems contain errors that are not found until the system has been in operation for many years. A better protection scheme would limit every segment's access rights to only those absolutely required for operation. In this scheme, segments that require certain access rights are issued "tickets" known as **capabilities.** In order to perform an object reference, the requesting segment must present the ticket that permits the appropriate reference. Capabilities are non-hierarchical protection mechanisms that allow software modules to access only the objects that they must access to perform their designated functions. Capability-based protection methods may be easily applied to all objects in a system if they are treated as segments (Chapter 5).

Since a link segment or access list is already associated with each segment, capability information can easily be added to these link segments. In this manner, link segments become **capability segments.** Each object descriptor specifies No Access, Read Only, Read/Write, and Execute Only. In addition, Read Capability, Read/Write Capability, and Copy Capability access rights are added. Capabilities and capability segments can only be created or deleted by a single highly-trusted task or function that contains the Write Capability access right. Capabilities may be copied and refined (deleting some access rights) by a task in order to pass capabilities on to less trusted subtasks. When copying a capability, a task may only refine (never increase) the original access rights.

The capability segment of a task defines the **protection domain** for that task. As demonstrated above, to share data it is necessary to grant two instruction segments (within a single task) different access rights to the same data segment. This function is accomplished by means of a special processor *enter* instruction that changes the current capability segment at the same time as a procedure is called. In this manner, a write access (to a shared data segment) is permitted only when specific procedures are executed. Although the calling program carries an alternate set of capabilities (to be used by these procedures), these capabilities can not be directly accessed by the calling program. These capabilities can only be used in conjunction with the *enter* instruction for a specific procedure instruction segment. On return from the procedure, the processor automatically restores the original capability segment(s), thereby restoring the original protection domain.

The ability to change protection domains in this manner permits a task to receive and transmit capabilities that it is not permitted to utilize directly. For example, a task wishing to perform I/O must possess an I/O capability. The task itself, however, is not permitted to utilize this capability; the task must pass the I/O capability to an I/O driver subroutine by means of an *enter* instruction. The I/O driver subroutine uses the capability to directly control the I/O device. On return, the capability is again hidden from the calling task.

User Profile

All task capabilities are derived from a master user capability list contained in a **user profile** maintained by system software. As capabilities are passed throughout the system, they actually reference the master capabilities within the user profile. This causes significant overhead the first time that a capability is referenced. Subsequent references may utilize a content-addressable capability store to eliminate the indirect reference overhead.

Computer systems communicate with the "real world" (external to the computer system) by means of **I/O interfaces**. An I/O interface permits a computer system to input data from, or output data to, **peripheral** devices such as CRT terminals, printers, tape drives, and disk storage units. **Input** is the term used to designate the process of bringing data into the computer system from external sensors. The input function may require translation of analog information into digital form. The term **output** specifies the reverse process, sending digital data from the computer system to external devices.

I/O Architecture

Computer systems may be designed to support various types of I/O interfacing techniques. Generally, there are two classes of I/O architecture, **direct I/O** (also termed **programmed I/O**) and **indirect I/O**. Direct I/O is an interfacing technique where a processor directly accesses I/O device registers by means of processor instructions. Most microprocessor systems utilize direct I/O facilities. Direct I/O may be **memory mapped** or **I/O mapped**. Input or output transfers that are accomplished by accessing I/O ports with special *INPUT* or *OUTPUT* instructions are said to be I/O mapped. I/O mapping requires separate address decoding and/or command signals for memory and I/O transfers.

Memory mapping provides I/O port registers that are addressed as if they were memory locations. Some I/O port registers addressed in this manner are *read only* or *write only* — although these registers are addressed as memory locations, they cannot be used with instructions that read and write the same memory location (e.g., increment memory). In fact, some hardware designs mate write only control data with read only status data in order to conserve memory addresses. In these implementations, reads and writes of the same memory location have no relation to one another.

Examples of both memory mapped and I/O mapped implementations may be found in many contemporary systems.

Chapter 9

Input and Output

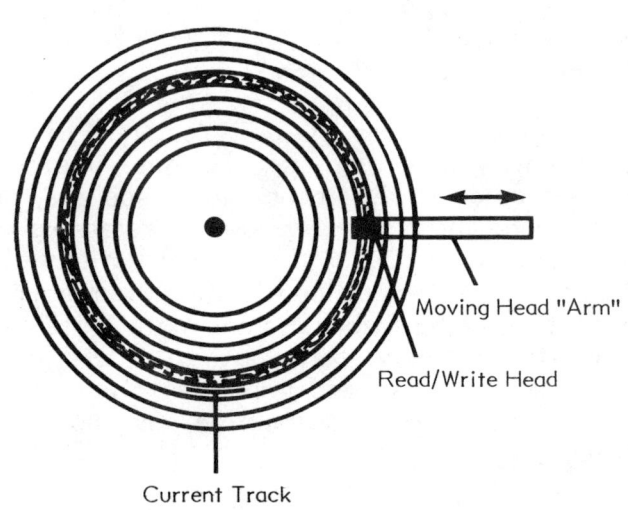

I/O Processors

Indirect I/O configurations place input and output operations under the control of an independent processing unit known as an **I/O processor, I/O channel,** or **peripheral processing unit** (PPU). An I/O processor is a special purpose processor that is dedicated to, and optimized for, input and output functions. I/O processors are designed to operate independently from, and simultaneously with, the general system processor. An I/O processor is typically used by software in the following manner:

1) A special I/O instruction area is set aside in memory by the task wishing to perform I/O. This area contains I/O instructions that cause the I/O processor to perform the required I/O transfers.

2) The task executes a *Start I/O* instruction that commences I/O processor execution of the instructions in the I/O area.

3) The task continues to execute on the system processor until it requires the I/O operation to be completed (e.g., when the task is ready to operate on the data read from a disk file).

4) The task executes an *I/O Wait* instruction that causes the task to stop executing until the I/O operation is complete.

5) Normal instruction execution is resumed after I/O is completed.

To effectively use an I/O processor, the software system must be structured in such a way that maximum parallel processing occurs. A multiprogramming operating system guarantees this capability since a task waiting for I/O can be suspended and another task can be executed. Without the support of a multiprogramming operating system, the task of keeping both processors busy becomes considerably more difficult. To effectively use an I/O processor without a multiprogramming operating system, a program generally starts I/O operations well before the data is actually needed and then proceeds to perform non-I/O operations in order to overlap processor execution.

I/O processors should always interface to the memory subsystem in the same manner as the system processor. I/O processors that do not observe the same addressing conventions as the system processor can pose serious software design problems. A common I/O processor implementation found in many contemporary systems requires the I/O processor to operate on physical addresses while the system processor uses logical addresses. In these implementations, a segment (or page) waiting for I/O cannot be relocated within memory or swapped to secondary storage since the I/O processor is only aware of the segment's current physical address.

I/O processors are generally divided into two categories based on their structure and use. A **multiplexer channel** is used with low speed I/O devices. Multiplexer channels concentrate data from many low-speed devices into one high-speed memory access channel. Data from the channels are time multiplexed (interleaved). A multiplexer channel is also known as a **concentrator**. A **selector channel**, on the other hand, is used in conjuction with high-speed I/O devices such as disk drives. Although more than one device may be attached to a selector channel, only one device can be serviced at a time.

I/O processors normally share the same data memory as the system processor by means of one of the following four access methods:

1) **DMA** - The processor is placed in a wait mode (usually called HOLD in microprocessor systems) while the I/O processor transfers data to or from memory at the maximum memory data rate. When the data transfer is complete, the processor resumes execution.

2) **Cycle Stealing** - Since memory cycle time is often shorter than processor cycle time, the I/O processor is synchronized with the system processor and the I/O processor steals memory cycles for data transfers between the memory cycles used by the system processor.

3) **Dual Port Memory** - If system memory units are designed with two complete data paths, both the system processor and the I/O processor may request memory cycles asynchronously. Since the memory can only perform one function at a time, dual port arbitration logic is designed to permit access on a first-come first-served basis with one port (usually the system processor) having priority in the case of simultaneous requests.

4) **Buffer Memory** - The I/O processor may have a local buffer memory where data from high-speed devices (hard disks or bubble memories) is stored temporarily until the I/O processor can acquire a data path to memory by means of one of the three previous methods.

Chaining

In systems containing an I/O processor, the software often builds lists consisting of multiple I/O requests. These lists are automatically executed in series by the I/O processor. This sequential I/O operation is called **chaining**.

Logical and Physical I/O

The wide variety of I/O devices available for today's computer systems makes it impossible for tasks to contain the instructions necessary to implement all of the required interfaces. The masking of physical I/O interface vagaries is one of the goals of good system design. To achieve this goal, physical device designations are replaced by logical names. These logical devices are **attached** to existing physical devices only when a task is executed. The ability for a task to reference logical devices (independent of actual physical devices) increases programming flexibility in the following ways:

1) I/O to an inoperative device can be reassigned to another identical device on the system.

2) I/O to a device currently in use (e.g., a printer) can temporarily be rerouted to a disk file (**spooling**).

3) During the software testing of a module, a programmer can attach all module I/O to a CRT terminal, although I/O will be routed to disk files in actual operation.

Software and hardware participates in the logical to physical mapping in a variety of ways as detailed in the following paragraphs.

Most systems force the logical to physical device translation onto the system software (operating system). In these systems, the operating system contains **device driver** modules containing the instructions necessary to interface with each valid physical peripheral device. When a physical device is attached to a logical device, the appropriate device driver is selected by the system to control the interface.

This software translation level can be supported in hardware if I/O devices are intelligent and each task utilizes an I/O device as if the device were another task. In this manner, I/O requests are indistinguishable from other messages between tasks. One of the tasks is simply an intelligent hardware I/O interface device. The advantage of this technique is uniformity. For example, to add I/O preprocessing, a new task is simply inserted between the I/O interface and the original requesting task. This new task now receives I/O requests from the original task and passes them on to the hardware. I/O responses are processed by the new task before they are returned to the requesting task.

A second method treats I/O devices as memory segments that have special attributes. I/O to these devices is system controlled (normally by hardware or microcode). The program uses these segments as if they were memory segments. For example, a CRT terminal would have read/write access rights while a printer would have write only access rights and a card reader would have read only access rights.

Parallel and Serial I/O

Most I/O interfaces can be characterized as serial or parallel. Parallel interfaces are capable of transferring data at very high speeds and are often used for disk I/O and inter-computer communication channels. Parallel interfaces transfer a complete data word in a single clock cycle. Serial interfaces, on the other hand, are slower, tansferring only a single bit each clock cycle. Serial and parallel interfaces may be synchronous or asynchronous as previously described in Chapter 6.

Parallel interfaces are generally more expensive than serial interfaces. Parallel interfaces require a wire for each bit of data transferred in parallel plus a clocking signal (e.g., 17 wires for a 16 bit word). A serial interface requires only two wires for the interface. Figure 9-1 illustrates typical serial and parallel I/O interconnections.

CRTs, Teletypewriters, and Printers

CRTs and teletypewriters are normally connected to computer systems by means of standard serial interfaces at the data rates listed in Figure 9-2. Low speed printers (e.g., daisy wheels) and moving-head dot matrix printers receive data over serial or parallel interfaces. High-speed line printers utilize parallel interfaces almost exclusively because of high interface speed requirements.

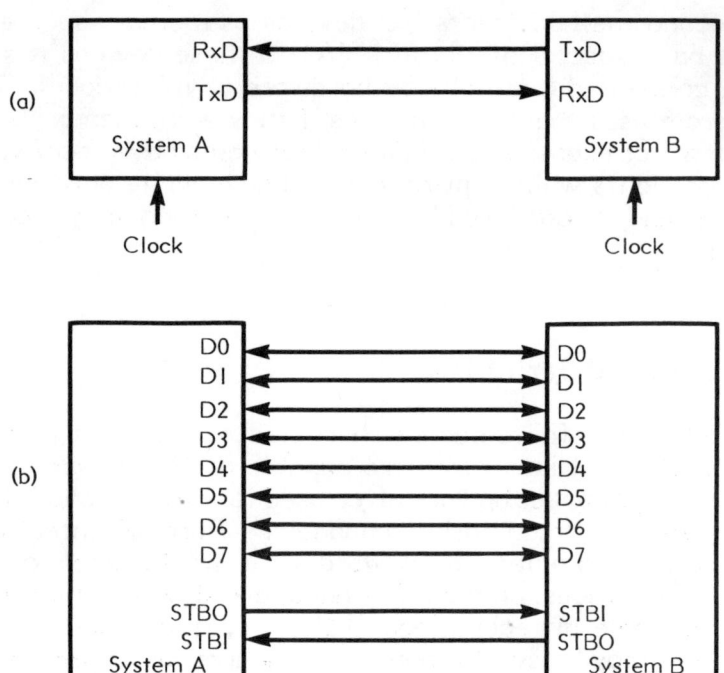

Figure 9-1 Serial and Parallel I/O Interfaces. The serial interface (a) transmits and receives data one bit at a time. Serial interface clocks may be identical (synchronous) or independent (asynchronous). The parallel interface (b) transfers one data byte at a time. A strobe signal indicates that the data is ready for transfer.

Magnetic Media

Magnetic media play a vital role in current computer systems. Flexible diskettes and moving-head disks provide large on-line data storage and filing capabilities, fixed-head disks (drums) and bubble memory devices are used for temporary high-speed swapping storage, and magnetic tape is used for archival storage.

Magnetic diskettes are circular pieces of flexible plastic covered with a magnetic coating and enclosed in a plastic

Transmission Baud Rates	Notes
110	Teletypewriters
300	Low-speed modems, teletypewriters
600	Low-speed modems
1200	Low-speed printers, CRT terminals
2400	CRT terminals, high-speed modems
4800	CRT terminals, high-speed modems
9600	CRT terminals, high-speed modems
19200	High-speed CRT terminals
38400	Intercomputer communication

Figure 9-2   Typical Serial Interface Data Rates.

jacket (Figure 9-3). Hard (rigid) disk platters (for moving-head and fixed-head disks) are fashioned of metal or rigid plastic coated with magnetic material. New magnetic media must be recorded with a fixed data **format** (by system hardware and software) before the media can be used to store data. Formatting is a method of adding information to the media that permits the system to read and write data without error.

The disk surface is divided into concentric circular **tracks** (Figure 9-4). A track is the area covered by a stationary read/write head in one revolution of the media. Diskettes, for example, normally contain 75 to 200 tracks. The amount of information stored on a track is a function of the recording density and the size of the track. For instance, IBM soft-sectored single density flexible diskettes store 3328 bytes per track.

A **sector** is an arbitrary division of a track. Sector size is determined by an analysis of system buffer size, disk access time and transfer rate, and total system storage capacity. Normally, sectors are fixed size disk blocks. IBM soft-sectored single density flexible diskettes allocate 26

Figure 9-3   A Magnetic Diskette.

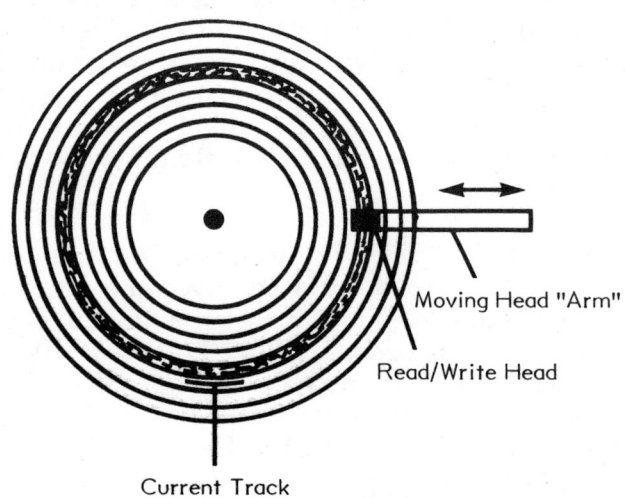

Figure 9-4   Concentric Tracks on a Disk Surface.

sectors to a track. Each sector stores 128 data bytes. Sector sizes on some disk devices are as large as four thousand bytes. In a paging system, efficiency considerations require that the page size be a multiple of the sector size. Figure 9-5 illustrates the IBM soft-sectored single density flexible diskette format.

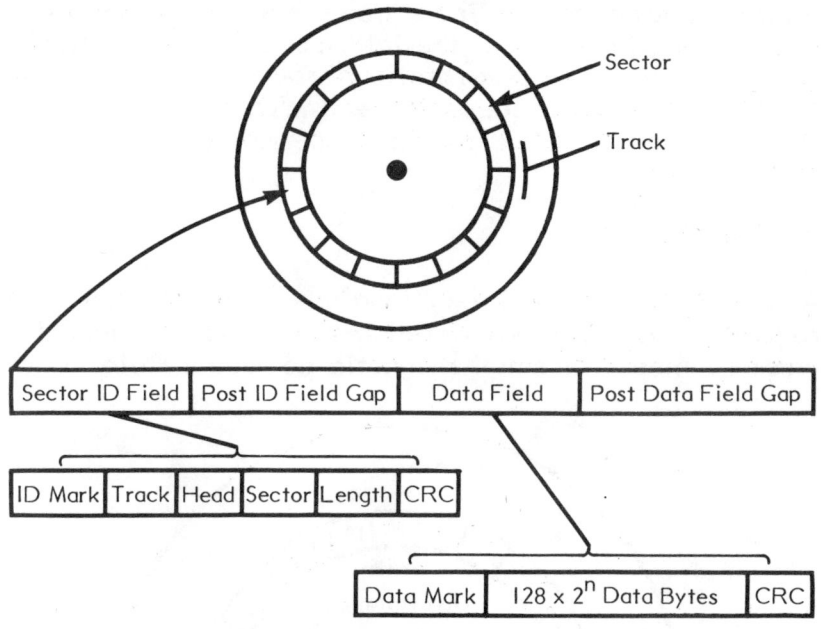

Figure 9-5   IBM Soft-Sectored Single Density Flexible Diskette Format.

Logical Sectoring

The initial formatting of a disk surface determines where logical sectors are located within a track. Some systems simply allocate logical sectors sequentially (mapping logical sectors directly into physical sectors). When multiple sectors are read and written, disk rotational timing is critical. After reading a sector, the processor may begin another I/O transfer for the next sector. Since the disk has continued to rotate, the next sector is already passing under the read/write head and the processor must wait for another complete revolution of the disk (10-100 milliseconds) before the sector read can begin. To improve performance, a technique known as **interleaving** is used. With this technique, logical sectors are not stored sequentially within a disk track. Instead, each logical sector is removed from the preceeding sector by a few physical sectors (known as the **interleave factor**) as shown in Figure 9-6. In practice, the interleave factor is initially calculated based on disk rotational speed and the average time between sequential sector reads. This initial estimate is then tuned to attain maximum performance from key system tasks.

Bubble Memories

A bubble memory is a very long non-volatile serial shift register. Data bits are stored within bubble memory devices by means of small magnetic domains. Rotation of

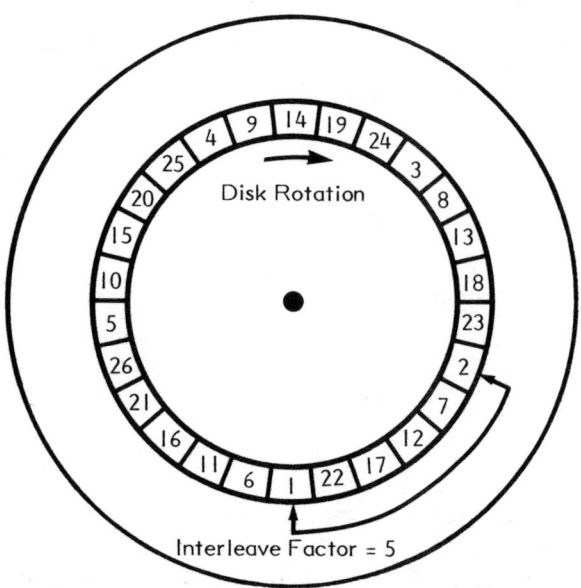

Figure 9-6   Interleaved Sector Allocation Within a Track.

an external magnetic field (by means of orthogonal coils) moves the magnetic "bubbles" along prescribed paths. A single bubble device approximately an inch square stores over one million bits of information. Internally, bubble memories are organized either as one long shift register or as multiple independent short shift registers (minor loops), all attached to another shift register (major loop). Figure 9-7 illustrates the major/minor loop memory organization. This second technique yields faster average access times to any location within the bubble memory since all minor loops can rotate simultaneously.

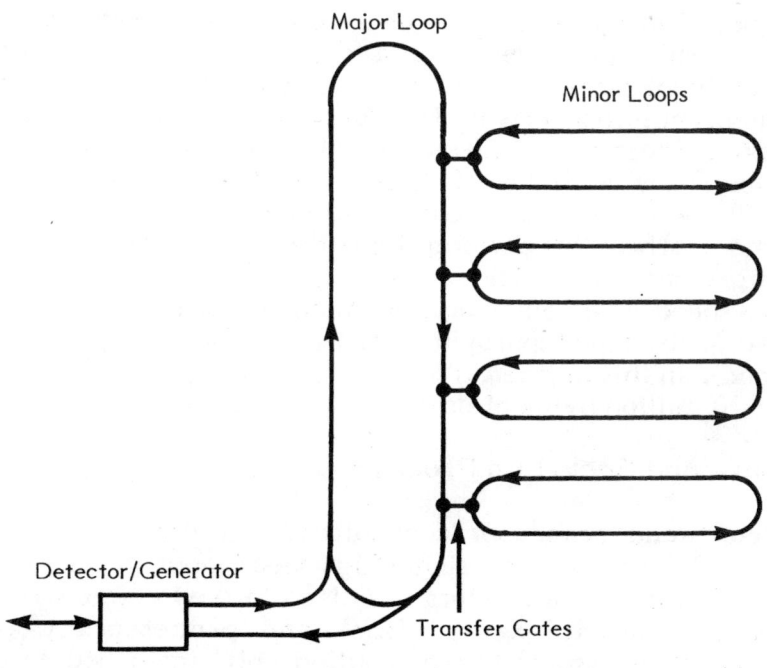

Figure 9-7   Major/Minor Loop Bubble Memory Organization.

Bubble memory devices may be used cost-effectively as low-power miniature fixed-head disks. Bubble memory storage is equivalent to an inertia-less fixed-head disk. While a fixed-head disk constantly rotates, bubble devices may be stopped and started at will. Initial positioning to a random data sector on either device requires approximately the same access time (8-10 milliseconds). Since bubble devices can be stopped and restarted with no delays, sequential reads require no additional access time, and interleaving considerations are not needed.

Magnetic Tape

Magnetic tape drives are similar to audio tape recorders. In the past, tape drives were used to store individual files for archival purposes and for on-line access. For these applications, tape drives were designed to start and stop quickly. These tape drives were often expensive and unreliable. Today, with the prices of sealed disk drives dropping rapidly, new low-cost tape drives are available for archival storage. These **streaming tape** drives are not required to start and stop quickly. Rather, once these drives are up to speed a complete disk dump occurs at the maximum speed of the tape (approximately thirty thousand bytes per second). In this manner, a small tape cartridge can contain over 10 million bytes of data.

Front- and Back-End Processors

A **front-end processor** concentrates and processes data from I/O sources into a single high speed input to the system. Front-end processors are often termed **concentrators** and **multiplexers**. **Back-end processors (Attached Processors)** are computing units (attached to a system) that process large quantities of data under control of, but independently from, the system processor. Data base processors and commercial floating point array processors are examples of back-end processors.

Chapter 10

Microprogramming

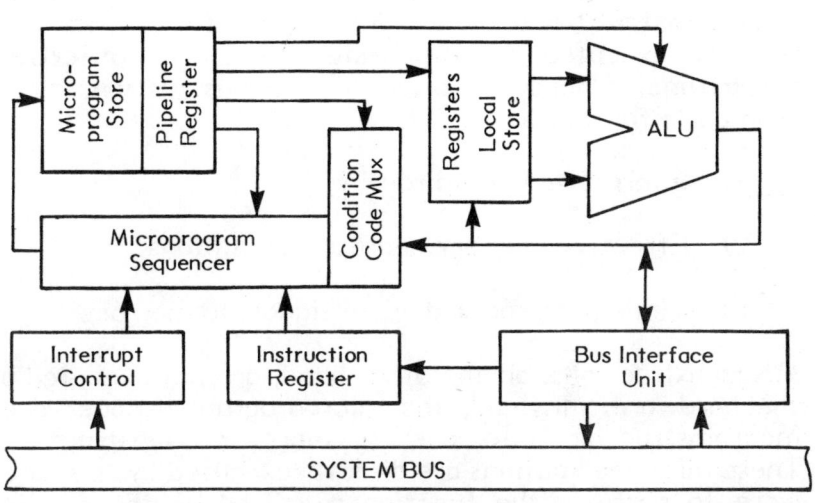

As computer system design evolved, proposals were made to structure new computer architectures in the same manner that software systems were structured. Proponents of these proposals argued that a more regular and highly flexible system design would be achieved if hardware operations and sequences were controlled by a low-level hardware-specific program (**microprogram**). Using this design technique, the intricacies of data transfers, of control signal timing, and of memory addressing were handled by executing microprogram instructions from a small, high-speed **control store.**

Microprogrammed system design has lived up to its initial claims. Today this design technique is so popular that most new processors and peripheral controllers are microprogrammed.

Macroinstructions and Microinstructions

In a microprogrammed machine, a distinction is made between the machine instruction set used by programmers (**macroinstructions**) and the instructions that are directly executed by the system hardware (**microinstructions**). Hardware oriented microinstructions direct such basic functions as:

1) Internal ALU data routing

2) Effective memory address calculations

3) Timing of read and write signals to memory

Macroinstructions, on the other hand, are not executed by the hardware. Instead, the microprogram decodes each macroinstruction into one or more microinstructions. These microinstructions are directly executed by the hardware to perform the function specified by the original macroinstruction. Figure 10-1 illustrates two simple machine instructions and their microinstruction equivalents.

```
MOV     R1,TBL(R2)      ---     Move the contents of a table (TBL), indexed
                                by register R2, to register R1.

        TRANS   MAR,PC          ; move PC to memory address register for instruction fetch
        ACT     RD              ; activate memory read signal
        WAIT    ACK             ; wait for memory acknowledge signal
        TRANS   IR,BUS          ; latch instruction into instruction register
        DEACT   RD              ; turn off memory read signal
        JUMP    IR(OPCODE)      ; jump to correct microcode for instruction opcode
          .       .
          .       .
          .       .

MOVOP:  TRANS   T,(IR(RB))      ; load temporary register with index register value
        ADD     T,IR(ADDR)      ; add table base address and index value
        TRANS   MAR,T           ; set address in memory address register
        ACT     RD              ; activate memory read
        WAIT    ACK             ; wait for memory acknowledge
        TRANS   IR(RA),BUS      ; move data into register specified in instruction
        DEACT   RD              ; turn off memory read signal
        JUMP    INSTLP          ; jump back to instruction loop to fetch next instruction


JMP     0400            ---     absolute program control transfer to
                                location 0400

        TRANS   MAR,PC          ; move PC to memory address register for instruction fetch
        ACT     RD              ; activate memory read
        WAIT    ACK             ; wait for memory acknowledge
        TRANS   IR,BUS          ; latch instruction into instruction register
        DEACT   RD              ; turn off memory read signal
        JUMP    IR(OPCODE)      ; jump to correct microcode for instruction opcode
          .       .
          .       .
          .       .

JMPOP:  TRANS   PC,IR(ADDR)     ; set PC to address contained in instruction
        JUMP    INSTLP          ; jump back to instruction loop to fetch next instruction
```

Figure 10-1 Equivalent Microinstructions for Sample Data Transfer and Control Transfer Macroinstructions.

Pipelining

As illustrated in Figure 10-1, it is often necessary to execute many microinstructions in order to perform one macroinstruction. For this reason, microinstruction execution is designed to be very fast; **microcycle** time is typically 50 to 200 nanoseconds. To achieve the fastest possible microcycle time, a technique known as **pipelining** is generally incorporated in all microprogrammed architectures. In a pipelined processor, the outputs of the control store are latched into a pipeline register.

These latches hold all the control information for the operations to be performed during the next microcycle. This allows access for the next microinstruction to be carried out during the actual execution of the current microinstruction. The next microinstruction is available from the control store at the end of the current microinstruction execution. In this manner microinstruction fetch and execute cycles occur in parallel, greatly shortening the microcycle time (often by 40 to 50%). Figure 10-2 illustrates microinstruction fetch and execute timing with and without pipelining.

Pipelining does have one drawback. Since the next microinstruction is being fetched during execution of the current microinstruction, conditional jump microinstructions must be delayed by one microcycle. This delay is necessary because the jump conditions cannot be evaluated until the current microinstruction has completed execution. In a pipelined design, the next microinstruction has already been fetched by this time, and it is too late to affect the execution of the next instruction.

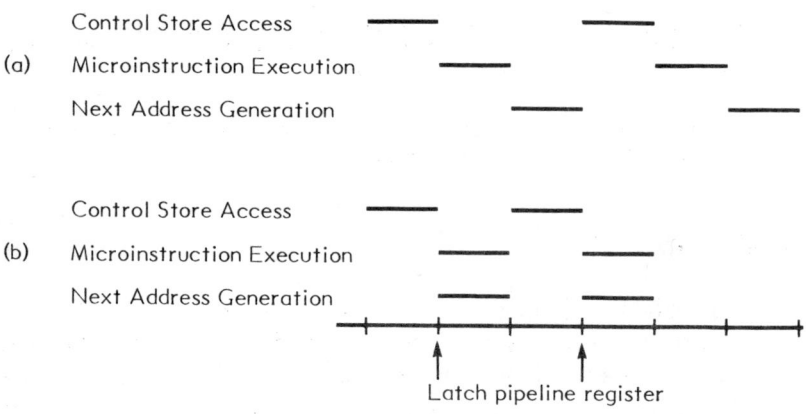

Figure 10-2   Microinstruction Timing: (a) without instruction pipelining and (b) with instruction pipelining.

Emulation

A microprogramming design philosophy results in CPU designs that are inherently very general purpose. The machine hardware is designed to perform only the basic functions required of almost all computer systems. It is the microprogram that sets one design apart from another. By changing/rewriting the microprogram, a processor can easily execute a different macroinstruction set — in fact it can be designed to execute the instruction set for other processors. This **emulation** feature of microprogrammed processors has been a popular way to capitalize on existing software. Often a company will upgrade an old computer system by designing a high-speed microprogrammed processor. The microprogram for this processor is designed to permit complete software compatibility with the old processor. In addition, new instructions are decoded by the microprogram so that the new processor has additional flexibility.

Horizontal and Vertical Microcode

When designing a microprogrammed processor, a decision must be made as to the number of independent functions to be simultaneously controlled by each microinstruction. The more functions that are controlled by an instruction, the longer the microinstruction word length.

Short word lengths (16-48 bits) permit only a few independent functions to be performed by each microinstruction. Complex operations implemented in this manner require a long sequence of microinstructions. This implementation technique is called **vertical microcode.** **Horizontal microcode** techniques use a wider word (56-400 bits) and perform many functions simultaneously. Vertical microinstructions tend to encode system command information in instruction fields, while horizontal microinstructions have individual gating control bits for each command (Figure 10-3).

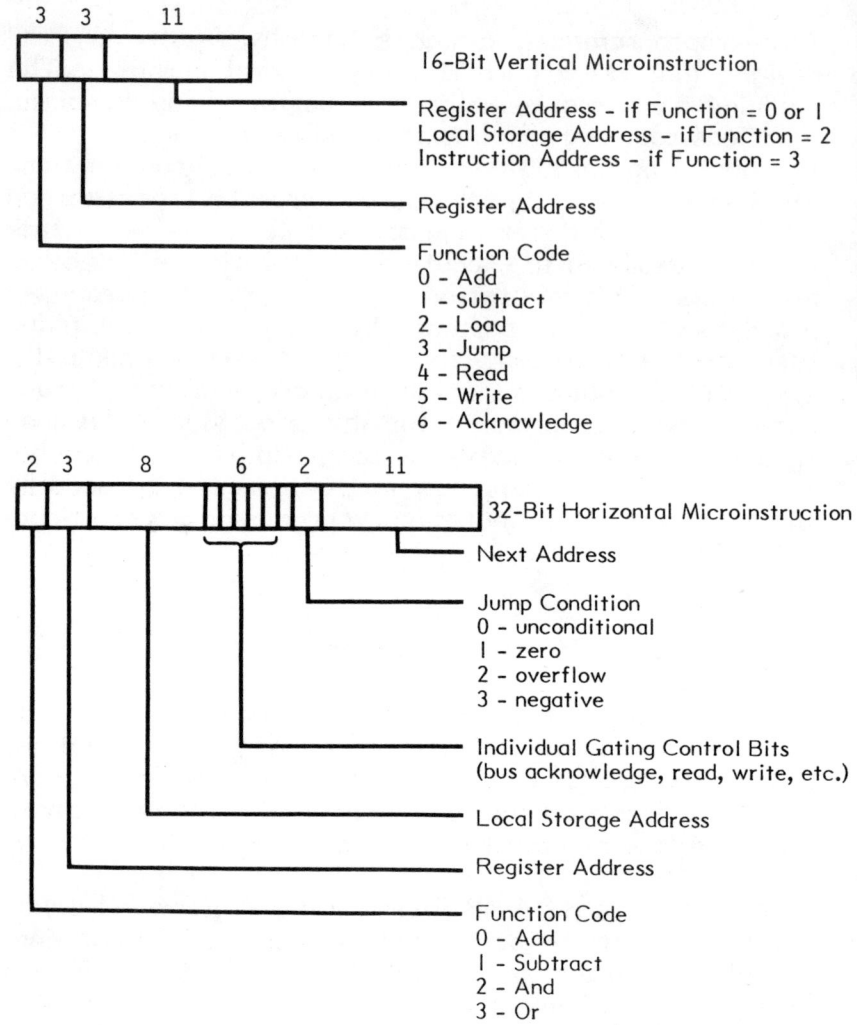

Figure 10-3 Typical Vertical and Horizontal Microinstructions. Vertical microinstructions encode fields to reduce microinstruction size. Horizontal microinstructions use separate fields for each function to maximize parallelism.

System Architecture

Generally, horizontal microcode is utilized when the microprogram is in direct control of all hardware functions (e.g. busses, gates, direct register transfers). Vertical microcode is used when the underlying hardware machine has automatic sequencing and decoding for many basic functions such as register transfers.

Some machines are designed to incorporate both types of microcode options. In these machines, the horizontal microcode is closest to the machine hardware, controlling internal gating, sequencing, and register transfer signals. This design level is referred to as a nanoprocessor and the nanoprocessor instructions are termed nanoinstructions. The next level of microcode is vertically oriented, decomposing into sequences of nanoinstructions. A macroinstruction within this architecture is first decomposed into a sequence of microinstructions, specifying machine actions (e.g., move register, access memory, etc.). Each of these microinstructions is in turn decomposed into nanoinstructions that carry out these actions (e.g., gate register to bus, float inputs, clock latch, etc.).

Writeable Control Store

The control store of most microprogrammed processors is composed of high speed read only memory (ROM) or programmable read only memory (PROM) with access times of 10-90 nanoseconds. Changing a microprogram in PROM or ROM is expensive and time consuming. To solve this problem, read/write random access memory (RAM) is often used to implement a **writeable control store (WCS)**. Unfortunately the cost of high-speed RAM severely limits the application of writeable control stores.

Writeable control stores are heavily utilized by microprogram design teams in order to easily change and test microprograms and microprogram modifications. Writeable control stores are also used to permit a machine to execute multiple instructions sets. Machines with WCS options can be dynamically optimized for particular calculations and/or applications. In conjunction with PROM/ROM, a small writeable control store also permits minor instruction set customization at reasonable cost.

Bit Slices

Since the microprogram is the customizing element in most microprogrammable architectures, it is natural to attempt to abstract common computer features and design standard LSI semiconductor devices to aid microprogrammable architecture implementations. Three basic components have been isolated: the control store memory, the arithmetic logic unit, and the microprogram sequencer.

The control store is implemented by means of high speed ROM, PROM, or RAM as described earlier. Both the arithmetic logic unit and the microprogram sequencer are normally designed to be configurable to various word lengths (in multiples of 2, 4, or 8 **bit slices**). Configurable bit slice components can quickly and easily be integrated to form complete processing units of 8, 16, 32, 64 bits or larger. Bit slices have introduced the advantages of LSI semiconductor technology (low cost, small size, and high speed) to custom designed processors.

Arithmetic and Logic Unit (ALU)

The computational heart of a bit slice processor is the Arithmetic/Logic Unit (ALU) and its associated register files. Normally, the same semiconductor device that contains the ALU logic also contains all or a portion of the register file (8 to 16 registers). Many ALU designs permit the register file to be expanded off-chip. A typical ALU device (Figure 10-4) contains the following components:

1) Function Decoder - Decodes microinstruction function codes into internal control and sequencing signals

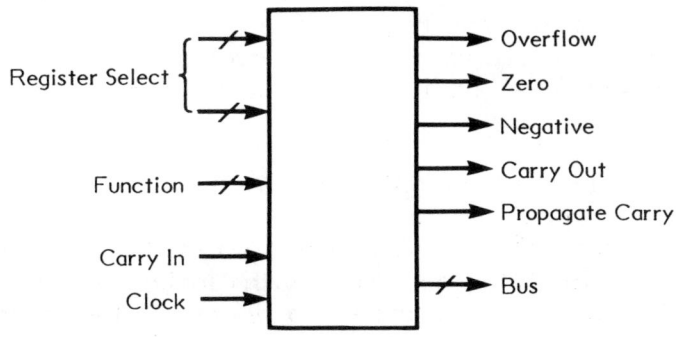

Figure 10-4   A Bit Slice ALU.

2) Arithmetic/Logic Hardware - Includes gates and control sequencers that perform arithmetic and logic functions (e.g., add, subtract, and complement).

3) Multiport Register File - High speed memory locations that are accessed for use in arithmetic operations. Normally two registers can be simultaneously read for a binary arithmetic operation (two port register file).

4) Input/Output Bus - One or more signal paths that permit data to be directly entered into, or retrieved from, the ALU.

5) Status Generation Logic - Provides discrete outputs for status signals such as overflow and carry.

The microinstructions for arithmetic operations specify data sources (register or bus), the operation code, the value of the carry-in flag, and result disposition (e.g., stored into the register file or output on the bus). A variety of status flags are available after an operation has been completed. Examples of status flags are:

1) Carry Out - Ripple carry to next ALU slice.

2) Propagate and Generate Carry - Carry information to be used with lookahead carry generators in order to increase the speed of arithmetic operations.

3) Overflow - A signal that arithmetic operations have overflowed the word size of the ALU.

4) Zero - An indication that the result of an operation is zero.

5) Sign - The top bit of the ALU slice indicating that the result of an operation is negative.

Carry Lookahead

The result of an arithmetic operation is not available from the ALU until the carry signals from each ALU slice have propagated through the entire ALU array. The carry-out signal from each bit slice can not become valid until after the carry-in signal is valid. The propagation delay from carry-in to carry-out is often 20 to 30 nanoseconds. For a wide word width, this carry propagation time can significantly slow operation time. Since carry operations are combinatorial, two output signals are generated within each bit slice (propagate carry and generate carry). The generation of these signals depends only on the arithmetic data and not on the value of the carry-in. Because they are independent of the carry-in and carry-out signals, the propagate and generate signals may be produced simultaneously by each bit slice element.

A combinatorial logic device known as a **carry lookahead generator** uses the carry propagate and generate signals to generate carry-in signals for all ALU slices within a very short time period (often less than 5 nanoseconds). One lookahead carry generator can be used with 4-8 ALU devices (depending on the design). Larger word widths may be accommodated with additional lookahead units at the expense of slightly longer delays. Figure 10-5 illustrates typical ALU connections with and without a carry lookahead device.

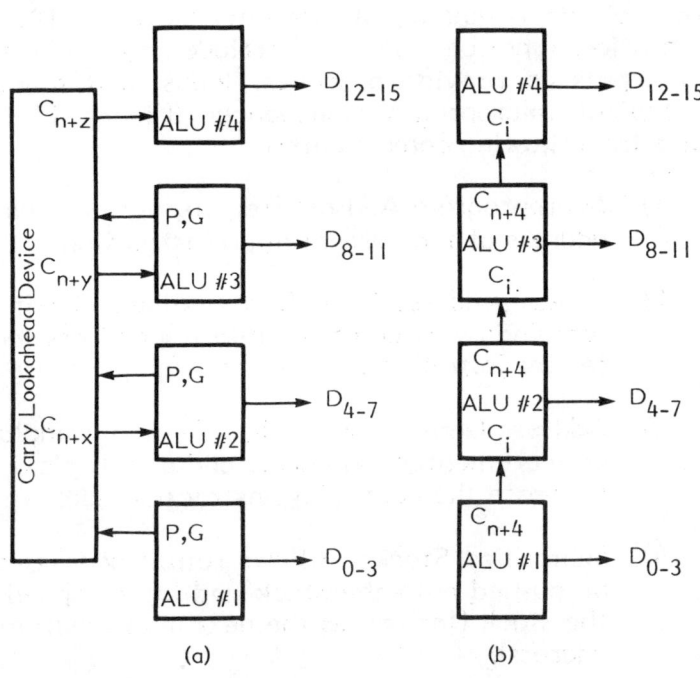

Figure 10-5 ALU Carry Logic: (a) with carry lookahead and (b) without carry lookahead.

Microprogramming

Microprogram Sequencer

Executing a microprogram is much like executing a standard machine language program. Execution flow must be controlled to provide loops, conditional and unconditional branches, and subroutines. The component that controls microprogram execution flow is the **microprogram sequencer**. The microprogram sequencer generates the addresses for control store fetches. While in the past sequencers have been designed with bizarre control flow characteristics, most commonly used devices today assume that microinstruction execution is sequential and the devices automatically increment the microprogram address at the beginning of each microcycle. This incrementation function can be overridden by other sequencer inputs to provide branches, loops, and subroutines. A typical microprogram sequencer (Figure 10-6) contains the following components:

1) Microprogram Address Register - Contains the address of the current microinstruction.

2) Direct Address Input Bus - Allows direct addressing override of the internal address register for initialization and interrupt response.

3) Address Generation Logic - Typically includes an incrementer, an adder, and a multiplexer to generate the next microinstruction address.

4) Subroutine Stack - Allows return addresses to be pushed onto the stack and later popped off the stack (for use as the next microinstruction address).

Interrupts and DMA

LSI devices have also been designed to support interrupt and DMA processing. Interrupt support devices permit the selective enabling, masking, and prioritizing of interrupt sources. Interrupt sources within a microprogrammed

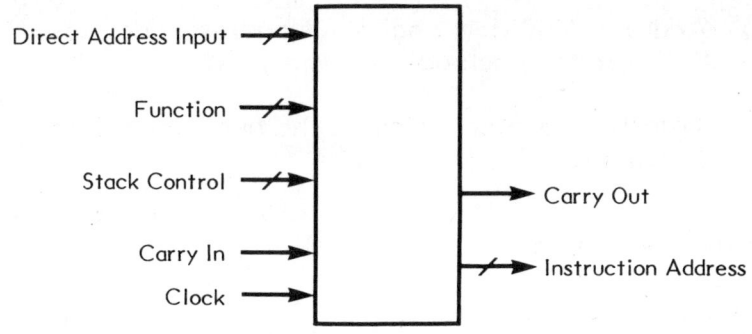

Figure 10-6 A Bit Slice Microprogram Sequencer.

processor are normally polled by the microprogram before the fetch cycle of each instruction. With this technique, recognition of an interrupt alters only the macroinstruction execution sequence of the processor. Interrupts recognized in this manner are termed **machine level interrupts**. At the designer's option, interrupts may directly alter the microinstruction execution sequence. In this design, a pending interrupt is recognized immediately after the current microinstruction is executed. This interrupt recognition method shortens interrupt latency but requires considerable attention during microprogram design. For example, microprogram sequencer stack space must be reserved and microinstruction loops must be designed to be easily resumed after a microinterrupt.

Specialized devices are also provided to support direct memory access (DMA). These devices may transfer blocks of data from memory to peripheral devices, from peripheral devices to memory, or from one memory location to another. The amount of data transferred may be prespecified or may depend on the actual data being transferred (e.g., transfer until an end of file character is sensed). DMA support devices contain the following components:

1) Address Registers - Contain memory and I/O addresses.

2) Address Modifier Logic - Updates addresses before/after each data transfer.

3) Transfer Counter - Counts the number of data transfers.

Bus Interface Unit

With the continued development of bit slice architectures, additional computer system functions may be isolated and translated into LSI components. The processor/bus interface is an example of an area where LSI design technology can be successfully applied. Most processors interface to a system memory bus or an I/O bus; processors in large systems often interface to multiple busses. Each bus may have its own transfer protocol (rules for interaction and data transfer). Obviously, the power of the processor would be optimized if a unit was specifically designed to support bus interfacing. **Bus interface units** are designed to programmably control bus transactions. These units contain the following elements:

1) Address Registers - Contain memory addresses for instruction, data, and stack segment accesses.

2) Address Generation Logic - Contains an adder/incrementer to produce instruction addresses and to perform relative address calculations.

3) Bus Interface Handshake Signals - Permits synchronous and asynchronous bus support at high speeds.

4) Bus Transceivers - Permit bidirectional data transfers between system I/O, memory, and processor busses.

5) Error Detection/Correction Logic - Detects and/or corrects bus transmission errors.

Chapter II

Error Detection and Correction

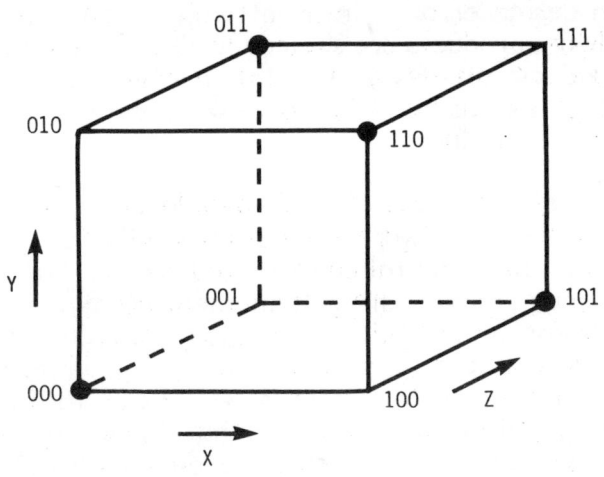

Original Data		Error Check Bit	Single Bit Error
X	Y	Z	
0	0	0	100, 010, or 001
0	1	1	111, 001, or 010
1	0	1	001, 111, or 100
1	1	0	010, 100, or 111

All systems experience errors. The object of good system design is to minimize the possibility for the occurrence of errors (**fault avoidance**), maximize the possibility of detection of errors (**fault detection**), and maximize the probability of operating in spite of errors (**fault tolererance**). The severity of system errors ranges from minor to devastating. For example, a harmless error occurs when a calculator fails to recognize a single keystroke, or when noise interrupts the transmission of a character from a word processing system to its printer. On the other hand, a malfunction in an intensive care life support/monitoring system can directly cause human death or disability.

Error Philosophies

The best design policy is always error avoidance. First and foremost, a hardware or software design should be free from design errors. In an attempt to enforce this policy, hardware products are subject to rigorous electronic analysis and circuit design simulation while software products undergo extensive design reviews, module testing, and acceptance testing.

As good as the goal of error avoidance is, past history has shown that hardware components will fail and software will inevitably contain undetected errors. With this understanding, each system implementation must establish a policy for dealing with errors. The simplest and least expensive philosophy ignores errors. This philosophy can be used only in the lowest cost systems (with little damage-causing potential). Designs that ignore errors are usually applied to tasks where a person directly interacts with the system and can spot incorrect results. Electronic toys, typewriters, and some computer aided design systems fall into this category. These sytems rely totally on the low failure rate of today's LSI microprocessor and memory components.

Once it is acknowledged that errors are expensive (in terms of money, reputation, and/or life), an obvious goal is the detection of errors before they can cause irreparable damage. Hardware error detection has been successfully applied to data transmission errors and memory errors, while software error detection is normally accomplished through the use of the protection strategies discussed in Chapter 8.

After an error has been detected, the system can:

1) Stop operating and request assistance (from a human operator or from a backup computer system).

2) Isolate the affected component(s), board(s), or software modules and continue operating.

3) Attempt to correct the error.

The first alternative is used in many critical application areas such as process control (e.g., refinery and nuclear power plant operation). The second alternative is used by many business transaction processing systems where constant system availability is required. The third option is generally restricted to subsystem applications (especially memory subsystems) where transient errors are common.

Hardware versus Software

By nature, hardware errors and software errors are significantly different. Errors may be classified as design errors, manufacturing errors, and field component malfunctions. Early in a system's life, hardware errors of all three types occur regularly. As system production matures, the first two error classes virtually disappear and the third class becomes predominant. Software errors, on the other hand, are all attributable to design errors. Software does not experience field component failures, and manufacturing errors (e.g., bad disk copies) are rare.

Another important difference between hardware and software errors is their dependence on external influences. After system installation, the probability of a hardware error in a given period of time reaches a steady-state level. Finally, after the system has been used for many years, hardware errors become more frequent and eventually the system must be replaced. In addition to this time dependence, hardware error rates also depend on environmental factors such as humidity, temperature, and dust levels. Software errors are not time dependent. Software quality does not degrade with system age. Rather, software errors depend on the system state and the system inputs.

Traditionally, hardware design has used standard well-defined and characterized building blocks (modules), techniques, and rules. Software design has always required customized modules. Hardware systems evolve slowly while software systems may be significantly redirected over night. Many people (both managers and software engineers) fail to recognize the true cost of software design since many aspects of the cost are insubstantial at design time (e.g., future maintenance costs). This difference is emphasized in the often-heard phrase "just write a little program." It's not often that the equivalent "just design a little board" is heard.

As a result of these fundamental design differences between hardware and software, software systems typically contain many more design errors when shipped to customers. Software emphasis must always be placed on releasing correct code (error avoidance). But, in any case, hardware and software errors are inevitable and good system design attempts to detect errors when they occur and ensure that these errors do not harm other parts of the system.

Hardware Errors

Hardware errors can be divided into single bit errors and burst errors. Single bit errors typically occur in memory subsystems where single storage devices may fail. Single bit errors are highly amenable to error correction. Burst errors occur during data transmission (to another system or to a peripheral device) and are caused by noise (electromagnetic interference). Burst errors in data transmission systems are detectable, but not easily correctable. Unfortunately, large amounts of data can easily be lost when a transmission channel is subject to noise.

To detect errors, every data word or transmitted message contains additional information that is used by the receiving device to check the integrity of the incoming data. Three methods are commonly used to encode this error detection information. The simplest method is **vertical redundancy checking (VRC)**. Vertical redundancy check procedures are applied to each character of data. Vertical redundancy checking (also known as **parity**) adds an extra bit to each data byte or character. The added bit is set or cleared to make the total number of "one" bits in the character even (even parity) or odd (odd parity). For example, the letter "A" is represented by the seven bit ASCII code 1000001. The VRC transmission code for this character contains eight bits; 01000001 for even parity and 11000001 for odd parity. Notice that a single bit error changes the received parity and is easily detected. Parity error detection techniques are often used to detect single bit memory subsystem errors. By adding a ninth bit to each data byte (12% memory size increase), single bit errors are easily detected. Parity methods do not detect double bit memory errors, nor do they offer error correction capabilities.

Another form of error detection code is the **longitudinal redundancy check** code (**LRC**). LRC checks are similar to VRC checks, but instead of adding a parity bit to each character, a parity check character (known as a **block check character** or **BCC**) is added to each message. LRC techniques check an entire message rather than a single character. This block check character is easily determined in hardware or software by simply computing the exclusive "OR" of all transmitted characters as shown in Figure 11-1. LRC checks have a higher probability of detecting burst errors than VRC checks. LRC and VRC codes are often combined in data transmission systems for higher reliability.

A **cyclic redundancy check** (CRC) is a more sophisticated and reliable method for checking the integrity of transmitted data. CRC strategies treat each message as a polynomial. Every "one" or "zero" in the message is a coefficient for an increasing power of a binary variable (X). X is used only to permit mathematical treatment and its value has no effect on the resulting check code. The message polynomial is divided by a predefined CRC polynomial (selected for its error detection capabilities) as shown in Figure 11-2. Standard CRC polynomials have been defined by international standards organizations such as ANSI, ISO, and CCITT. CRC-16 and CRC-CCITT (used in the SDLC data transmission protocol) are two common CRC polynomials.

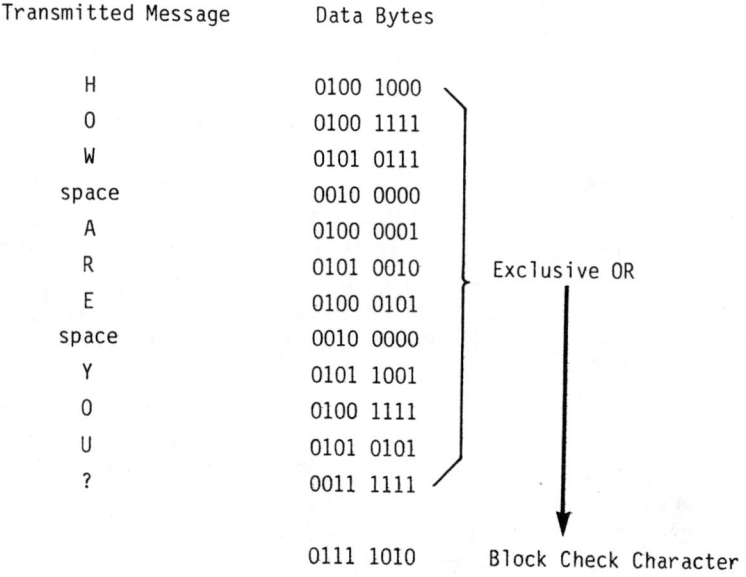

Figure 11-1   An LRC Block Check Character Computation.

Transmitted Data	"a"	0110 1000	$x^6 + x^5 + x^3$
CRC Polynomial		0001 0101	$x^5 + x^3 + 1$
Check Character (remainder)		0001 0011	$x^4 + X + 1$

Division:

$$\begin{array}{r} X + 1 \\ x^5 + x^3 + 1 \overline{\smash{\big)}\, x^6 + x^5 + x^3 } \\ \underline{x^6 + x^4 + X } \\ x^5 + x^4 + x^3 + X \\ \underline{x^5 + x^3 + 1} \\ x^4 + X + 1 \end{array}$$

Figure 11-2   A CRC Computation.

Block check characters are normally appended to the end of a message transmission. As the data is received, the receiving device performs an identical block check calculation. When the message is completed, the internally computed block check character is compared with the check character found in the message. If an error is detected, the system typically attempts to retransmit the message. Continued transmission failures indicate a component or data link failure.

Error Correcting Codes

Today, considerable use is made of **error correcting codes** (notably **Hamming codes**) that correct n-bit errors and detect n+1-bit errors. The operation of error correction codes is best understood by imagining all possible values of a data element as vertices on a polygon. Without error detection or correction, all vertices are separated by one edge and a single-bit error will change one

Error Detection and Correction

legal value into another. Error detection codes operate by adding extra bits to data elements so that all valid values (vertices) are separated by one invalid value (vertex) as shown in Figure 11-3. When a single bit is altered, the original valid value is translated along one side of the polygon to an invalid vertex. When this translation occurs, the new vertex is known to be invalid and the error is detected. This error cannot be corrected because it is midway between two valid vertices.

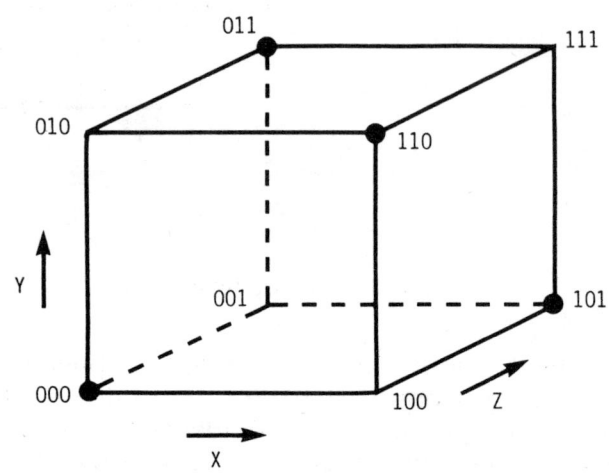

Original Data		Error Check Bit	Single Bit Error
X	Y	Z	
0	0	0	100, 010, or 001
0	1	1	111, 001, or 010
1	0	1	001, 111, or 100
1	1	0	010, 100, or 111

Figure 11-3 Error Detection on a Two-Bit Data Word by adding an additional data bit. Note that all valid vertices of the cube are separated by one invalid vertex. A single bit error moves a valid value to an invalid vertex.

By adding additional bits, the valid vertices can be separated by two invalid vertices (three sides of the polygon). A single bit error translates the data value to an adjacent invalid vertex (thus detecting the error). The error is corrected by noticing that the new vertex is closer to one valid vertex than to any other. To correct one-bit errors and detect two-bit errors, the distance between any two valid vertices is increased to three invalid vertices. With this separation, two errors will cause the modified data value to land on an invalid vertex, halfway between two valid vertices. Three or more errors could land on a valid vertex and be undetectable.

Software Errors

Since software modules usually contain some errors even after careful testing, it is critical to provide error detection capabilities that are enforced as the software executes. The system architecture cannot predict the correct actions of a program, but actions by software modules that violate the modules' capabilities can, and should be, detected and prevented. This rationale is the basis for the resource protection mechanisms discussed in Chapter 8. Normally a software module has the capability to use only specified hardware resources (e.g., a specific section of memory or a specific I/O port). Two architectural concepts that assist software error detection are tagged data structures and object/capability-based addressing. In both cases, data structures are treated as objects that can only be referenced by means of well-defined access algorithms. In addition, each object has specific parametric limits that can be tested automatically by the system hardware to verify the integrity of the program module.

Faults

Hardware errors are often termed **faults**. The term fault is also used to indicate any event that is out of the ordinary and often implies events that are expected but whose timing is unknown. Faults include:

1) Interrupts - asynchronous **events** (see Chapter 6).

2) Exceptions - software error conditions.

3) Hardware Errors - Component failures.

4) Virtual Control - Page replacement, access right requalification, software traps, and single step operation.

Exceptions may be divided into the following classes:

1) Mathematical - Arithmetic overflow, underflow, domain errors (e.g., the square root of a negative number), and attempted division by zero.

2) Addressing - Stack overflows and underflows, illegal memory references, and protection violations.

3) Control - Attempts to execute privileged instructions and unimplemented operations.

4) Data Access - Attempts to use undefined data and invalid vector and array subscripts.

Fault Handling

Faults cause the system to discontinue normal task processing and perform other services. Most systems handle faults automatically and immediately. The best system designs integrate fault handling into the normal task scheduling process. Operating systems generally perform these fault handling functions.

When a fault is detected, the system has at least four processing options:

1) Automatically Correct and Continue - Faults such as arithmetic overflow and underflow often specify system default handling procedures. For example, a floating point underflow may set the result to zero and continue processing.

2) Retry - This option is used for bus errors, memory errors, and page faults, where the fault is expected to be a transient occurrence. The faulted task is typically suspended while the fault handling procedure is invoked.

3) Execute Task Fault Handler - When a module or task expects possible faults, the module may specify procedures or tasks to be executed in the event that the fault occurs. The system simply passes fault information to this fault handling software.

4) Terminate Execution - In the event that no fault handling algorithms are available for a particular fault, the faulted module is terminated. The fault is then passed on to the procedure or task that called (or initiated) the faulted module. This termination and fault passing procedure continues until a task or module is found to deal with the fault.

Most current systems specify a single fault handler task for each fault (normally a dedicated memory location to which control is transferred when the fault occurs). Operating systems may provide a more general structure at the expense of large software overhead.

Watchdog Timer

Many systems contain a system-wide error indicator called a watchdog timer. The timer is retriggerable and is set for an interval between 10 and 100 milliseconds. Periodically (every time the operating system is entered) the timer is retriggered. If the system software fails to retrigger the timer (indicating a serious system malfunction) the timer automatically restarts the system and generates the appropriate alarms.

Power Fail and Auto Restart

Most systems also contain a mechanism to protect the system in the event of a power failure. When the "power line low" signal is sensed by the power supply, a high priority interrupt is generated. Software saves critical data in non-volatile memory (core or battery backed-up RAM). When power returns, the system is automatically restarted where it left off.

Appendix A

Glossary of System Architecture Terms

Absolute Addressing - Another term for Direct Addressing.

Absolute Code - Machine instructions in which physical addresses are determined at language translation (assembly or compile) time.

Accept - A system communication and synchronization primitive that permits a task to extract a message from a mailbox. The task is not suspended if the mailbox is empty.

Access List - Another term for a Linkage Segment.

Access Path - The environment (conditions) under which an object is referenced. Access path protection mechanisms allow the same object to be protected in different ways depending on the environment in which the object access is attempted.

Access Rights - A list of objects or segments that may be accessed by a software module. The list includes the allowable operations on each object (e.g., read, write, or execute).

Access Time - The amount of time required to fetch a given data element. This time may be as short as 25 nanoseconds for data in a cache memory buffer or as long as hundreds of milliseconds for a flexible diskette sector access.

Accumulator - A high-speed storage location (normally in the processor ALU) that contains data used in arithmetic or logic operations. The results of these operations usually replace the previous data in the accumulator. Many architectures (especially small minicomputers and microprocessors) contain a single accumulator; others allow any register (within the working register set) to be used as an accumulator.

Acknowledge - A signal returned to a processor or computer system to indicate that a requested operation has been completed.

Address - A description of the location of information within a computer memory (storage) subsystem.

Address Map - Specification of the logical to physical address translation.

Address Space - A set of data storage locations, all of which are accessed in a similar manner by software modules. Some architectures define more than one address space — commonly separating program memory and data memory. Special instructions may be required to access separate address spaces.

Addressing Mode - The manner in which an effective address is calculated by a processor. Common addressing modes are direct, immediate, indexed, indirect, register, and relative.

Allocation - The process of setting aside a system resource for use by a requesting task.

Algorithm - Specification of an information processing procedure.

Architecture - The definition of the structure and organization of an information processing system.

Argument - Another term for a Parameter.

Arithmetic-Logic Unit (ALU) - The portion of a processor that performs arithmetic operations (e.g., add, subtract, multiply, and divide) and logic operations (e.g., AND, OR, and XOR) operations on data contained within a computer system.

Array - A n-dimensional data structure equivalent to a mathematical matrix.

Array Processor - A processor containing multiple ALUs to efficiently perform parallel calculations on array/vector elements.

Glossary

ASCII - Abbreviation for American Standard Code for Information Interchange. This code permits electronic systems to transmit and receive text. Each character (e.g., a, x, P) is assigned a number between 32 and 127. These numbers are easily transferred electronically between systems.

Associative Memory - Another term for Content-Addressable Memory.

Asynchronous - A term describing two or more events or signals that have no fixed relationship in time. Asynchronous operation is often found in communication protocols and in computer system designs where a master clock is not used.

Attach - Substitution of an existing physical device for a logical device reference.

Attached Processor - Another term for a Back-End Processor.

Back-End Processor - A computing unit that processes large quantities of data under the control of, but independently from, the main system processor.

Backing Store - Another term for Secondary Storage.

Backplane - A printed circuit bus implementation. System modules interface to the bus by means of sockets mounted on the printed circuit backplane.

Bandwidth - The maximum data transmission rate of a bus or communication data link.

Bank Switching - A method of extended addressing that permits each system task to occupy a "bank" of physical memory. Each bank of physical memory is equal in size to the complete logical address space of the system. To implement this technique, three or four address bits (8 to 16 banks) are added to each memory reference. Each task/user has its own bank address.

Base Register - A high-speed storage location that contains the address of the first data word or instruction of a segment. All addresses within the segment are referenced to the start of the segment, and during execution, the physical address of each memory reference is calculated by adding the contents of the base register to the relative addresses contained within the segment. Sector relocation is accomplished by simply moving a segment in memory and placing the new address in the base register.

Baud - The number of times per second that the state of a transmitted signal (on a data link) can change. When the transmitted signal has only two states, the baud rate is equal to the bit rate.

BCD - An abbreviation for Binary Coded Decimal. BCD representation is used to store decimal numbers in binary form. Each BCD digit requires 4 bits of data storage.

Best Fit - An algorithm for memory allocation that searches the memory free list for the unused memory block that is closest in size to that requested.

Binary - 1) Base two numbering system. Binary digits (bits) only have two values: 0 and 1. A binary number is represented as a sequence of bits representing increasing powers of 2. For example, 10110 = 1*16 + 0*8 + 1*4 + 1*2 + 0*1 = 22. 2) An operation that requires two operands, e.g., addition and subtraction.

Binding - The process of fixing the position of logical addresses within the physical address space.

Bit - A single binary digit. A bit of information has only two states: 0 and 1 (OFF and ON).

Bit Map - A representation of allocated and free sectors on a disk that is used to increase the performance of secondary storage management algorithms. The bit map consists of a block of single bit flags (one bit for each sector on the disk volume). A set bit indicates that the corresponding sector is allocated; a cleared bit indicates that the corresponding sector is free.

Bit Slice - A processor building block. Each bit slice device operates on a fixed number of bits (2, 4, and 8 are common). Multiple devices are connected in parallel to perform operations on complete data words. For example, four 4-bit slices are used to perform operations on 16 bit data words.

Block - Another term for a Page Frame.

Block Check Character (BCC) - A character (or group of characters) that is appended to a message for use by a receiving device in checking the integrity of the transferred information.

Block Transfer - The ability to move multiple data words from one location within a computer system to another location (in the same or a different system). Block transfers are often used to move tables of data within memory or between an I/O device (e.g., a disk drive) and memory.

Branch - 1) A common term for a conditional or unconditional control transfer instruction or the physical act of changing the normal sequential instruction execution flow of a processor. 2) Connection between the nodes of a tree data structure.

Buffer Memory - A high speed local memory area that is used by I/O processors to store transmitted and/or received data. Normally, buffer memories are used either because a peripheral device has higher speed requirements than memory can support or because additional processing must be performed on the data by the I/O processor (either before or after transmission).

Bus - A connection among modules within a computer system over which commands, addressing information, and data are transferred. A hardware bus is composed of multiple electrical conductors (often a multiconductor cable or printed wiring board backplane). Standardized calling sequences, parameter passing conventions, and communications protocols can be thought of as components of the software bus.

Bus Interface Unit - A processor element that controls bus interface protocols.

Busy Wait - A situation in which a task waits for access to a resource by continuously testing a flag. Although the task is not performing useful work during its wait, the processor is busy (executing test instructions) and no other task can execute on that processor.

Byte - A data element consisting of 8 bits. A byte can represent unsigned integers between 0 and 255 or signed integers from -128 to 127.

Cache - A small but very high-speed memory buffer situated between the processor and main memory in a computer system. This buffer operates on the principle that certain memory locations tend to be accessed often (normally for reads). When a main memory location is read, it is stored in the cache at the same time. Further read references to this location are automatically routed to the cache. A write access usually writes to both main memory and the cache. Since a cache represents many noncontiguous main memory locations, content-addressable registers are used to determine when a main memory location is currently duplicated in the cache. One problem that arises with a cache has to do with the handling of I/O channels that can write into main memory without the processor's knowledge. In order for the cache to be correct at all times, all write accesses to main memory must be monitored.

Call - The process of transferring control to a procedure (subroutine or coroutine) for the purpose of performing a predefined function or calculation.

Calling Program - A software module that calls (invokes) a procedure (subroutine or coroutine). The calling program may itself be a procedure called by another software module.

Calling Sequence - The actual instruction sequence required to call a procedure and pass the necessary parameters.

Capability - A protection mechanism that allows software modules to access only the objects required to perform their designated functions. A capability is a "ticket," issued by the system, that must be presented by a module when requesting access to objects.

Capability Segment - A segment that contains capabilities and may only be modified by a few operating system programs.

Card Cage - The combination of a backplane (printed circuit board bus) and electronic module mounting hardware.

Central Processing Unit (CPU) - The portion of a computer system (also called a processor) containing the ALU and system control hardware. The CPU usually fetches an instruction and then executes that instruction (by performing a set of predefined operations on data stored within the system). Most systems contain a single CPU, but the recent proliferation of microprocessors has led to an increase in the number of multiprocessor system designs.

Chaining - The capability of an I/O processor to execute lists of software generated I/O requests.

Character - Data elements (six to eight bits) that store coded alphanumeric characters and punctuation. ASCII and EBCDIC are examples of commonly used codes.

Checkpoint - A periodic data base dump of critical information that permits a backup processor (in a dual processor configuration) to take over processing duties in the event that the primary processor fails.

Communication - The capability of a computer system to transfer information to another system. Communications support requires specialized hardware and software. The hardware controls the electrical signals connecting both systems, while the software ensures that information is transferred in a compatible format without error.

Communication Primitives - System functions that permit tasks to send messages to, and receive messages from, other tasks.

Concentrator - Another term for a Multiplexer Channel.

Consumable Resource - A resource (e.g., message) that is produced (filled) by one task and consumed (read and acted on) and freed by another task.

Consumer - A task that uses a consumable resource.

Content-Addressable Memory - A memory that is addressable by contents rather than by location. For instance, instead of reading the data at location 453, data is read from the location that contains the string "BETA" in the upper 32 bits. Content-addressable memories (containing recently-used segment base addresses) are often used in segmented systems to

Glossary

improve performance. Segment names and base addresses are paired in memory locations. To access the segment "ALPHA", all memory locations are simultaneously searched for "ALPHA". This typically occurs within 25 to 100 nanoseconds. If "ALPHA" is found, the next data value can be loaded into a base register for a segment access. Without a content-addressable memory, the segment table must be accessed for each segment reference.

Context - The body of changeable information that belongs to a task. This information must be saved when a task's execution is suspended so that the task may be restarted later without error. Context information typically includes the contents of the processor registers, the program counter address, and the processor, I/O, and interrupt status.

Context Switching - The process of saving the context of the currently executing task or user and restoring the context of some other task within the system This process is normally associated with interrupt processing. Context switching is a very time consuming process for most systems since processor status and the contents of the processor registers must be saved. To facilitate context switching, many systems automatically save the current instruction address and the processor status in memory when an interrupt occurs. Other systems contain multiple register sets that can be swapped (by means of a single instruction) to avoid the overhead required to store registers in memory.

Control Store - Microprogram storage (usually very high-speed ROM/PROM) in a microprogrammed processor design.

Coprocessor - A processor that operates in conjunction with other processors within a computer system. Coprocessors may be complete CPUs operating in a tightly coupled multiprocessing environment or they may be special purpose processors (e.g., I/O processors and arithmetic processors) that share timing and control functions with the main system processor.

Critical Section - A portion of software that accesses a shared resource and must be protected so that other tasks are not permitted to simultaneously access the same resource. For example, when updating a 32-bit floating point number, all four bytes must be written before another task may read the data.

Cycle - This term is commonly used to describe three separate items. 1) An instruction cycle refers to the sequence of operations (and the time) required to read an instruction and perform the desired operation. An instruction cycle is often divided into a fetch cycle (to read the instruction into the control unit) and an execute cycle (to perform the desired operations). 2) A clock cycle refers to the timing of a system oscillator. Instruction cycles normally consist of multiple clock cycles. The number of clock cycles in an instruction cycle varies from instruction to instruction (and may also be a function of the data on which the instruction operates). 3) A memory cycle refers to the minimum time required between memory access requests.

Cycle Stealing - A memory access technique in which an I/O processor is synchronized to the general processor's memory cycle timing in such a way that it "steals" memory cycles between those used by the general system processor. This memory interface technique is used in systems where the memory cycle time is significantly shorter than the processor execution cycle.

Cyclic Redundancy Check (CRC) - An error checking technique that provides a high degree of error detection. CRC methods are often used in data transmission and peripheral I/O systems where burst errors are frequent.

Daisy Chain - A type of communication network or bus configuration in which all devices are connected together serially. The first device is the master. Communication from the network manager to any other device must pass through all devices between them.

Data - Coded information within a computer system.

Data Encryption - A means of scrambling information to be transmitted between systems in order to protect proprietary data. Only another system with a "key" to the encryption code can decipher the information.

Data Link - An interface between two or more computer systems that permits one of the systems to transmit data to, and to receive data from, another system.

Data Stream - A sequence of data that is operated on (in a serial manner) by a processor.

Data Structure - A mechanism, including both storage layout and access rules, by which information may be stored and retrieved within a computer system. Data structures may reside in primary or secondary storage. Matrices of numerical data and data files are common examples of data structures.

Decision Tree - A data structure used to automate complex decision making tasks. Each node of a decision tree contains the specification for a test operation. Branches (one for each valid test outcome) lead from this test node to additional test nodes or to a termination of the testing process.

Demand Paging - A paging algorithm in a virtual storage system where a page is not loaded into physical memory until a reference is made to that page.

Device Driver - A system software module that supports logical to physical device mapping by directly controlling data transfers to and from I/O peripherals.

Direct Addressing - An addressing mode in which the effective address is contained in the instruction and no address calculations are performed.

Direct I/O - A facility, usually specified as part of the computer system architecture whereby input from, or output to, peripheral devices is performed under direct processor control by means of special I/O instructions. For example, *OUTPUT the ACCUMULATOR to PORT X* is a direct I/O instruction. Most microprocessors support direct I/O.

Directory - A data structure containing entries for each file within the file system. Each directory entry contains information about the corresponding file such as: name, owner/creator, access rights, size, and location. Directory entries may also be pointers to subdirectories.

Dirty Bit - A bit flag contained in each page table entry that indicates whether the corresponding page frame in primary storage has been altered since it was moved from secondary to primary storage. The dirty bit is reset whenever a page is loaded into primary storage and set when a data word within the page is written.

Dispatcher - Another term for the Scheduler.

Distributed Intelligence - A design philosophy that utilizes microprocessors extensively in all system devices. These microprocessors permit each device to perform traditional roles (with additional features) and also to communicate information to other "intelligent" units.

Distributed Processing - A multiprocessing technique in which each processor has a specific task or set of tasks to perform. These processors transfer commands and data by means of a standard communication interface. In some cases, programs are transferred between processing units. However, the transfer of programs is normally utilized only for power-on loading and control algorithm changes rather than Load Sharing.

DMA - An abbreviation for Direct Memory Access — a memory access technique in which the system processor is placed in a wait mode (usually called HOLD in microprocessor systems) while another device (e.g., an I/O processor, I/O peripheral, or coprocessor) transfers data to or from memory at the maximum memory data rate. When the data transfer is complete, the system processor resumes execution.

Dual Port Memory - A memory subsystem design that provides two complete paths (address, data, and control) into the available memory space. This technique permits two processors (usually a general processor and an I/O processor) to request memory cycles asynchronously. Since the memory can only perform one function at a time, dual port arbitration logic is designed into the memory subsystem to permit access on a first-come, first-served basis, with one path (or port) having priority during simultaneous requests. In practice, dual port memory designs provide significantly higher throughput because memory cycles are almost always significantly shorter than processor cycles.

Dyadic - An operation that requires two operands, e.g., addition and subtraction.

EBCDIC - An abbreviation for Extended Binary Coded Decimal Interchange Code. This code permits electronic systems to transmit and receive text; each letter, numeral, and punctuation mark is assigned a code number that can easily be transferred electronically between systems.

Effective Address - The address of data to be used during the execution of an instruction. The effective address is often the result of complex address calculations specified by the addressing mode of the instruction in combination with the underlying addressing architecture of the system.

Emulation - The capability of a microprogrammed processor to execute the instruction set (and all available software) of another computer system.

Entry Point - 1) The starting point of a task (predefined by the programmer). 2) The beginning of a subroutine.

Error Correcting Code - A data encoding that permits data errors to be detected and corrected. Error correcting codes add redundant information to each data value. If errors are present, this redundant information isolates the error and contains sufficient information to correct the error.

Event - A condition used to synchronize system operation. A peripheral or timer interrupt, the occurrence of an exception condition, and the arrival of a message from a software module are examples of events.

Event Flag - A synchronization mechanism that is used to coordinate the execution of two cooperating tasks.

Exception - A software error condition. Arithmetic overflows and protection violations are examples of exceptions.

Execute Cycle - The portion of an instruction cycle during which arithmetic and logic operations are performed as specified by the current instruction code.

Exit Point - The ending instruction of a subroutine that returns control to the calling program.

Extended Addressing - An addressing technique that permits the physical address space to be larger than the logical address space. This technique is often used to allow physical memory expansion of existing systems. Extended addressing translates logical addresses to physical addresses by adding a physical memory offset to each logical address. The ability to alter the physical memory offset (for each task or segment) is reserved for use by the operating system.

Extended Processing Unit (EPU) - Another term for a Coprocessor.

Fault - A computer system event that is out of the ordinary during normal system operation. Faults include interrupts, software and hardware errors, and virtual control interruptions such as page replacement and access right requalification.

Fault Avoidance - The attempt to avoid hardware and software errors by careful system design and testing.

Fault Detection - Mechanisms and techniques by which hardware and software errors may be detected and isolated when they occur.

Fault Tolerant - Computer system design techniques that guarantee continued system operation and integrity in the face of hardware and software errors.

Fetch Cycle - The portion of an instruction cycle during which the next instruction is loaded into the processor and decoded.

FIFO - An abbreviation for First-In First-Out.

File - A named segment (collection of data) stored on secondary storage media.

Firmware - A method of system control program design in which all control instructions are contained in ROM or PROM. Firmware based systems have the same advantages as software based systems (notably flexibility) but are less expensive.

First Fit - An algorithm for storage allocation that searches the free list only long enough to find an unused memory block that is large enough to satisfy the storage request.

First-In First-Out (FIFO) - A data access mechanism that implements a queue. Data elements are always extracted from the data structure in the same order that they are entered (the first element in is the first element out).

Fixed Point - Rational decimal number representations with a fixed number of decimal places to the right of the decimal point.

Floating Point - A number representation used for scientific calculations. Floating point numbers contain a fixed number of significant digits within a large dynamic range.

Format - Initialization of secondary storage media with information necessary to assure that data can subsequently be read or written without error. The information is usually closely related to the read/write hardware. A common example of a popular formatting technique is the IBM soft-sectored format for single density diskettes.

Four-Address Instruction - An instruction that contains four addresses: the addresses of two operands, the address in which the result is to be stored, and the address of the next instruction to be executed. Many microprogram instructions are four-address instructions.

Fragmentation - The division of contiguous storage area (e.g., main memory or disk storage) in a way that causes areas to be wasted. For example, allocation of variable sized memory blocks from a fixed pool will cause small areas of memory to become unusable. At the point where this wasted space impacts system performance, Garbage Collection is performed.

Friendly Environment - A software environment in which no hardware protection mechanisms are available. All software must be adequately tested to ensure that tasks will not interfere with one another.

Front-End Processor - A processor that concentrates and processes data from multiple I/O sources into a single high-speed input to a computer system.

Full Duplex - A data link over which information can be transmitted in two directions simultaneously.

Garbage Collection - The process of reallocating fragmented storage in such a way as to reclaim wasted space. Garbage collection is a drastic and time consuming operation that is only invoked when storage utilization is extremely low and is seriously affecting system performance.

Gate - A well-defined and tightly controlled entry point into a protected system function.

Generalized Address - An address consisting of three components: a segment number, a page number, and a page offset.

Graceful Degradation - Performance degradation in a fault tolerant system after one or more component failures. Although no functionality is lost, speed and efficiency may be sacrificed.

Grant - A signal generated by the system controller in response to a *request* signal issued by a processor module or I/O device. For example, a disk drive may generate a bus request. When the previous bus cycle ends, the system controller grants the bus to the disk drive in order to transfer data to memory.

Half Duplex - A communications data link over which data can be transmitted in two directions, but not simultaneously.

Hamming Code - A common error correction code used in memory subsystem designs.

Handshake - A method of controlling data transfers in which the transmitting device or system generates a *data ready* signal. This signal directs the receiving device to accept the data. The receiving device then generates a *data accepted* signal, informing the transmitting device that it may remove the data and proceed.

Hard Error - An error in magnetic media, electromechanical devices, or electronic circuits that is repeatable.

Hardwired - A system control unit in which all control logic is discretely wired and soldered into the system. Modifications to correct errors/malfunctions or to upgrade these systems are costly and time-consuming.

Horizontal Microcode - A method of microprogram design that increases the number of functions that can be performed simultaneously (by a single microinstruction) by adding specialized unencoded control fields to each microinstruction (widening the microprogram control words). Microinstruction widths of 48 to over 100 bits are common.

Huffman Coding - The most efficient instruction encoding. Instruction probabilities are used to generate a unique series of variable bit length codes. With Huffman coding, often used instructions have the shortest op codes; seldom used instructions have long op codes. This coding ensures efficient use of program memory storage space.

Immediate Addressing - An addressing mode in which the data (to be used during instruction execution) is contained within the instruction stream. Systems with large word sizes (24 bits or more) normally fit immediate data into the lower 8 or 16 bits of the instruction word. Systems with small word sizes utilize one or two bytes sequentially following the operation code to contain the data.

In Circuit Emulation (ICE) - A capability provided on many microcomputer development systems that enables a system designer to use the facilities of the development system to debug prototype hardware and software. Physically, this is accomplished by means of an umbilical cable from the development system that plugs into the microprocessor socket in the prototype system.

Index Register - A register containing a memory offset or table index (used to compute the effective address) in the indexed addressing mode.

Indexed Addressing - An addressing mode in which the effective address is calculated by adding the address data contained in the instruction to the contents of an index register. Indexed addressing is extremely useful when accessing sequential tables of information. In this case, the instruction contains the address of the first data word in the table. The index register contains the "index" (or memory offset in bytes or words) of the desired table item.

Indirect Addressing - An addressing mode in which the address contained in the instruction is not the effective address. To compute the effective address for an instruction utilizing indirect addressing, the processor must first read the data contained in the specified memory location. This data is then used as the effective address and a second memory access must be performed to read or write the data).

Indirect I/O - A facility, usually specified as part of the computer system architecture, whereby input from, or output to, peripheral devices is performed by a unit separate from the main processor. This unit is commonly called a Channel or I/O Processor.

Input - The process of bringing information into the computer system from external sensors (peripherals).

Instruction - The specification of a computer operation (e.g., addition or subtraction) and the data on which the operation is to be performed.

Instruction Cycle - The sequence of operations required to read an instruction and perform the desired computations. An instruction cycle is often subdivided into a fetch cycle (to read the instruction into the control unit) and an execute cycle (to perform the computations).

Instruction Lookahead - A method of processor operation that prefetches instructions from memory before previous instructions have been executed. Prefetched instructions are entered into a queue (often limited to 2-16 instructions) in the processor. Addresses for the memory fetches are generated by incrementing the program counter. The processor queue must be flushed (emptied) whenever a control transfer (e.g., JUMP or CALL instruction) is executed.

Instruction Pointer - Another term for Program Counter.

Instruction Prefix - An instruction modifier code that temporarily overrides standard system defaults during instruction execution.

Instruction Register (IR) - A register in the control unit of a processor or CPU into which an instruction is placed after it has been fetched from memory. This register is used for instruction decode and control generation during the execute portion of the next instruction cycle.

Instruction Set - The collection of all valid instructions executable by a processor. Instruction sets are usually unique to a given processor although well-known architectures have spawned innumerable "plug-compatible" copies and upgrades.

Instruction Stream - A sequence of instructions that is executed (in a serial manner) by a processor. An instruction stream is also called a Process.

Integer - Representations of whole numbers (no fractions) used to count and monitor indivisible items.

Interleave Factor - The number of physical sectors between one logical sector and the next logical sector on a disk track.

Interleaving - A track formatting technique utilized with moving and fixed head disk media in which logical sectors are not stored sequentially. Instead, each logical sector is removed from the preceding sector by a few physical sectors. Using this technique, multiple sectors may be read or written sequentially with a minimum of disk latency.

Interrupt - A signal that causes a processor to suspend operation of the currently executing software (as soon as possible — typically after execution of the current instruction) and to transfer control to special interrupt handling software. Interrupts are used to signal conditions that require immediate and special handling. Exceptions such as an arithmetic overflow or a divide by zero normally generate interrupts. In addition, external devices such as disk and tape drives generate interrupts to signal the completion of an operation or to signal an I/O error.

Interrupt Latency - The time delay between the occurrence of an interrupt and the beginning of interrupt processing. Interrupt latency includes interrupt recognition time plus context switching time.

Interrupt Vector - An ordered set of memory locations that contains the addresses of interrupt service routines. When an interrupt occurs, the processor determines the interrupt code and uses this code as an index into the interrupt vector. In this way, the correct interrupt service routine address is determined and control is automatically transferred to the service routine.

Intersegment Reference - An access to data or instructions within a segment that was initiated within a different segment.

Interval Timer - A hardware or software clock that generates an interrupt after a specified period of time has elapsed.

I/O - An abbreviation for Input and Output — the interaction of a computer system with the external environment.

I/O Channel - An I/O processing unit that controls all input from, and output to, peripheral devices in computer systems. A channel frequently has its own instruction set dedicated to I/O operations. After initialization by means of operating system software, programs need only execute *START I/O* instructions to perform complete I/O transactions. In most system architectures, channel processors operate in parallel (concurrently) with the general purpose system processor, significantly increasing system throughput.

I/O Interface - Hardware and software that permits a computer system to input data from, or output data to, the external environment by means of peripheral devices. I/O interfaces are also called peripheral interfaces.

I/O Mapped - A method of implementing system input and output (to peripheral devices such as CRT terminals and disk drives) that provides special *INPUT* and *OUTPUT* instructions. This mapping separates the memory address space from the I/O address space. I/O mapping requires separate hardware address decoding for memory and I/O transfers.

I/O Processor - Another term for an I/O Channel.

Job - A collection of cooperating tasks used to solve an information processing problem.

Known Segment Table - A segment table containing descriptors for all segments referenced by a task or system.

Least Recently Used - A page replacement technique that replaces the page that has been unused for the longest period of time.

Length Register - A register that is used in conjunction with a base register in task security implementations. The base register contains the lowest physical address of a segment. The contents of the base register plus the contents of the length register is the highest physical address of the segment.

Line Switching - A network communication method that operates in a manner similar to a public telephone. To transmit a message from one network node to another, all required data links must be reserved by the transmitting node. A message is then transmitted over this path. While the transmitting node retains control over the individual data links, no other node may use these data links.

Line Turnaround Time - The data link idle period during which the direction of data transmission (on a half-duplex data link) is reversed.

Linear Addressing - A method of effective address calculation in which the segment number may be altered by the addressing calculations.

Link - A pointer (contained in each element of a linked list) to the next item within the list.

Linkage Segment - A task segment that contains an identifier for each external segment accessed by the task.

Linked List - A data structure in which each element contains a pointer to its predecessor or successor (single linked list) or both (doubly linked list).

Linking Loader - A system software program that connects previously assembled/compiled modules into a unit that can be loaded into memory (at a specified address) and executed.

Load Sharing - A technique used in multiprocessing systems where a task (when ready to execute) will be run on the next available processor. In order to make this technique operate successfully, all processors must be identical and have identical memory addressing capabilities.

Logical Address - A method of addressing data and/or program instructions in such a way as to be independent of the physical memory structure of a given computer system. For example, a logical address may be specified as WORD 5 OF SEGMENT ALPHA. Of course, when the program executes, the logical address is translated by either hardware or software into a physical address within the physical memory space.

Logical Address Space - The program's (and programmer's) view of system storage.

Longitudinal Redundancy Check (LRC) - An error detecting code that adds a block check character to each transmitted message. This check character is computed from the characters within the message and is checked by the receiving device to ensure message integrity.

Looping - Repeated execution of an instruction sequence.

Loosely Coupled - A multiprocessor configuration in which each processor contains its own system software and performs tasks in a semiautonomous manner, utilizing local memory and local peripheral devices. Processors in this configuration are connected by a central bus or by a communications data link.

Machine Instruction - A coding (usually a binary pattern, e.g., 01011001) of a processor instruction that can be directly executed by the processor hardware.

Machine Level Interrupt - An interrupt that is recognized on the macroinstruction level rather than on the microinstruction level. Machine level interrupts cannot interfere with the execution of a macroinstruction; machine level interrupts are recognized *between* macroinstructions.

Macroinstruction - An instruction contained in the machine instruction set used by programmers. In microprogrammed designs, macroinstructions are not directly executed by processor hardware; macroinstructions are interpreted by a microprogram.

Mailbox - A system data structure that is used for task communication. Tasks send messages to, and receive messages from, Mailboxes.

Master - A unit in a computer system that controls communications functions.

Memory - Another term for the primary store.

Memory Address Register (MAR) - A register within a processor used to generate the effective address for the next memory access. The MAR is not usually available to the programmer; it is controlled by the system hardware or microprogram.

Memory Manager - A combination of system hardware and software that manages the physical memory resource and controls memory allocation for tasks in the system. In a virtual memory or paging system, the memory manager also translates logical addresses into physical addresses and implements the page fetch, placement, and replacement algorithms.

Memory Mapped - A method of implementing system input and output (to peripheral devices such as CRT terminals and disk drives) that permits the I/O devices to be accessed as if they were memory locations.

Memory Protection - An architectural feature that prevents a software module from interfering with the execution of another module. Interference is prevented by permitting access only to specified memory segments. If a module attempts to access data outside of the specified segments, a protection violation interrupts execution while the operating system takes appropriate action.

Message - A unit of communication between tasks and/or system processors.

Microcomputer Development System - A system designed exclusively to aid in the development of microprocessor systems. Microcomputer development systems enable a designer to develop software and hardware as if many standard system utilities were present in his final design. However, these utilities actually reside in the development system and therefore do not require costly additions to every shipped system.

Microcycle - A microinstruction cycle of a microprogrammed processor.

Microinstruction - An instruction that is directly executed by a microprogrammed processor.

Microprocessor - A small and inexpensive silicon integrated circuit that functions as a CPU or complete computer system. Microprocessor systems are generally more cost-effective and more flexible than previous hard-wired logic designs.

Microprogram - A program (sequence of microinstructions) for a microprogrammed processor.

Microprogrammed Processor - A processor (often designed with bit slice components) where random logic control elements are replaced by a regular and flexible control structure. This control structure is contained in ROM/PROM memory as a set of microinstructions. Each microinstruction directly controls the operation of the processor latches, interconnection buses, status words, and memory address computations. Every machine instruction is composed of multiple microinstructions that fetch the instruction, decode it, compute the effective addresses, perform memory reads to fetch data from the effective addresses, control the arithmetic-logic unit (to perform computations), and write the result to the correct storage locations.

Microprogram Sequencer - A bit slice component that controls microinstruction execution flow.

MIMD - An abbreviation for Multiple Instruction stream, Multiple Data stream architecture. This architecture contains independent parallel processors that execute more than one task simultaneously.

MIPS - An abbreviation for Million Instructions Per Second.

MISD - An abbreviation for Multiple Instruction stream, Single Data stream architecture. In this architecture, a single data element is processed simultaneously by multiple independent instructions/ALUs.

Module - A section of software that has well-defined inputs and outputs and may be tested independently of other software.

Monadic - An operation that requires only a single operand (e.g., complement).

Multidrop - A type of communication network in which all devices are connected together on a single data link. Each device has a unique address on the data link, and any device may communicate directly with any other device attached to the link.

Multiplexed Bus - A bus design in which address and data are time multiplexed over the same set of electrical conductors.

Multiplexer - 1) A device that selects and transmits one of n inputs to a receiving device. Multiplexers may be used to attach multiple processors to a shared bus or memory unit. 2) A unit that concentrates input (to a central processor) from multiple I/O devices (especially low speed terminals and data links).

Multiplexer Channel - An I/O processor that concentrates data from many low-speed I/O devices into one high-speed memory access channel.

Multiport Memory - A memory subsystem design that provides two or more paths (complete with address, data, and control signals) into the memory. This technique permits multiple processors to request memory cycles asynchronously. Since the memory can only perform one function at a time, multiport arbitration logic is designed to permit accesses on a first-come, first-served basis, with one path (or port) having priority for simultaneous requests. In practice, multiport memory design provides significantly higher throughput because memory cycles are considerably shorter than processor cycles.

Multiprocessing - The capability of a system to support multiple processors.

Multiprogramming - The capability of a computer system (usually through its operating system) to support multiple tasks (software modules) that run concurrently.

Multitasking - Another term for Multiprogramming.

Nesting Depth - The maximum number of subroutines in progress at a given time. For example, if module A calls procedure B and procedure B calls procedure C, the nesting depth is 2. If C returns to B and B calls D, the nesting depth is still 2. If D calls E, the depth increases to 3.

Network - A data communications system consisting of multiple computer systems and data links.

Nibble - A 4-bit data element.

Node - An intelligent unit within a data communications network.

Non-Von Neumann Architecture - An architectural design that differs from Von Neumann's original linear, homogeneous, and sequential memory. For example, designs that separate program (instruction) memory from data memory or designs employing tagged data are non-Von Neumann.

Normalized - A data representation technique for floating point numbers in which the topmost bit of the fraction (or mantissa) is always set. This technique eliminates multiple representations for the same data values and increases computational accuracy.

Object - A data structure whose internal storage representation is not visible to software modules that access the object. Valid operations on objects are carefully defined and controlled by the system.

Object-Addressing - An addressing method in which the programmer specifies the object name and the required operation to be performed. The programmer does not need a detailed understanding of the object's physical implementation.

Object Code - The output of an assembler or compiler that executes on a processor. Linking and loading may be required before this code can execute directly on the processor.

One-Address Instruction - An instruction that contains only one operand address. When the instruction is executed, the data at this address is used. The result of the instruction is either stored at this address (as in the case of a COMPLEMENT MEMORY instruction) or the result is assumed to reside in the accumulator (as in an ADD X instruction). The address of the next instruction is not explicitly specified in a one-address instruction; the next instruction is assumed to begin at the address immediately following the address of the current instruction.

One-Level Store - A method of storage management that treats all storage levels identically. All data is stored in named segments. These segments may (at a given time) reside in primary or secondary storage. The programmer is not aware of the actual location of these segments; the system invisibly provides all necessary segment management.

Ones Complement - A representation method for binary integers used in some computer systems. In ones complement representations, the sign of a number is changed by a logical complement operation. A ones complement representation has the disadvantage of two distinct representations for zero.

Op Code - Another term for Operation Code.

Operand - A data input to, or a result of, an operation.

Operating System - A collection of system software that permits user tasks to interface to machine hardware and interact with other tasks in a straightforward, efficient, and safe manner.

Operation Code - The portion of an instruction that specifies the operation to be performed (e.g., Add, Subtract, And, Or).

Output - The process of sending digital data from a computer system to peripheral devices in the external environment.

Packet Switching - Transmission of messages from one network node to another by dividing each message into one or more fixed size information packets. Whenever a node receives a packet that is not addressed to it, the node temporarily stores and subsequently retransmits the packet over the best available data link. To transmit a message, the source node simply formats a set of packets (containing a destination code) and transmits these packets to a neighboring node (in the general direction of the destination node). Each intermediate node sends the packets toward their destination over the best path.

Page - An artificial division of physical memory in order to facilitate memory management in multiprogramming systems. Pages are normally fixed size memory blocks between 512 bytes and 4096 bytes in length.

Page Fault - A condition that occurs when the logical address referenced by a task is not currently available in physical memory. At this point, a special algorithm is executed that finds the page containing the referenced address, determines where to locate it in physical memory, swaps out any page required to place the new page in memory, loads the page into memory, and finally returns control to the faulted software module.

Page Frame - A block of physical memory corresponding to a page of logical memory.

Page Table - A table of page information contained within each segment. Each page table entry contains the current physical address of the corresponding logical page, a validity flag (to determine if the page is currently loaded into physical memory), and a dirty bit (indicating whether the page has been altered since it was moved into physical memory).

Paging - A physical address space management technique that divides the logical address space of a segment into fixed size pages. Pages may be moved into and out of memory as required without impacting the operation of software modules. Paging is invisible to the programmer.

Parallel - A technique that increases data processing speed (by incorporating multiple processors) or data communication speed (by transmitting multiple data bits simultaneously).

Parallel Processing - A technique for increasing system throughput by combining multiple ALUs within a processor and/or by combining multiple processors within a system. ALUs and processors within the system can operate in parallel (simultaneously).

Parameter - Information passed between a procedure and its calling program.

Parity - A vertical redundancy check technique used extensively for memory error detection. Parity implementations add an extra bit to each data byte. This bit is set or cleared based on the number of "one" bits within the byte. If a single-bit error occurs, the parity bit is no longer correct and the error is easily detected when the data byte is read.

PC Relative Addressing - Another term for Relative Addressing.

Performance Monitoring - System support software and/or hardware used to measure the performance of a computer system by timing and recording the execution of various tasks and modules. This timing information is then used by system analysts to tune the system for maximum efficiency by modifying system hardware and/or software.

Peripheral - An electronic or electromechanical unit such as a line printer, CRT terminal, card reader, or paper tape punch that is attached to a computer system.

Peripheral Processing Unit (PPU) - Another term for an I/O Channel.

Physical Address - The address of an existing system memory location.

Physical Address Space - The actual physical implementation (the system's view) of addressable data storage.

Pipelining - A mode of computer operation in which independent operations are overlapped. Pipelining can be implemented in any system composed of independently functioning modules. When one module has completed its function, the results are passed on to the next module "down the pipe." The original module is then free to perform its function a second time with new data. A typical application of pipelining involves overlapping the fetch and execute cycles within a processor. After the instruction fetch unit has passed the decoded instruction on to the execution unit, the fetch unit begins the fetch for the next instruction (even though the previous instruction has not completed execution). Pipelining is also used to advantage in vector operations. If an operation to be performed on a 1000 element vector requires 10 microseconds, but can be partitioned into 10 discrete and independent one microsecond steps, a new element can be piped into the processor every microsecond (all previous elements advance one step). Therefore, the complete vector can be processed in 1010 microseconds — almost ten times faster than it could be processed without pipelining.

Pointer - A data element containing the address of another data element or of a data structure. When a pointer is used in a data access, the system automatically uses the address in the pointer to locate the data. In many systems, addressing flexibility is obtained by permitting pointers to reference other pointers.

Polling - An event synchronization technique in which software periodically samples an input to determine if a relevant event has occurred.

Pool - A reserved memory area from which memory space (for messages and I/O buffers) is allocated. All allocated memory is returned to the pool after use; memory space may be reallocated after it is returned to the pool.

Position Independent Code - Executable code that runs (without modification) independent of the physical memory location at which it is loaded. Position independent code either contains only relative transfer instructions, or all addressing is done by means of base registers.

Prefetching - The operation of fetching an instruction or data value before it is actually needed by a processor.

Primary Store - Another term for memory — high-speed system storage that can be randomly addressed for single read or write transfers.

Privileged Instruction - An instruction that affects the security of a computer system and may only be executed in the privileged execution mode. Set Interrupt Mask, Load Base Register, Load Protection Register, and Start I/O are examples of privileged instructions.

Privileged Mode - A mode of processor operation in which privileged instructions may be executed. Many computer systems execute in one of two modes: user and privileged. System software executes in the privileged mode and may execute all processor instructions; user application software executes in the user mode.

Procedure - An independent software module (instruction sequence) that is designed to perform a single function. Procedures are "called" as required by other executing software modules to perform the specified function.

Process - Another term for a task.

Processor - A device that can execute the instructions of a task. A processor executes one task at a time.

Processor Status Word (PSW) - A processor register that contains processor status information. Typically processor status consists of the results of the last arithmetic or logical operation (e.g., carry/borrow, overflow, and zero flags), the interrupt status (enabled/disabled), and the memory bank number.

Producer - A task that generates a resource used by another task.

Program - A sequence of instructions written to perform a specific function.

Program Counter (PC) - A processor register that contains the address of the next instruction to be executed. The program counter is automatically incremented by the processor (as instructions are executed) and modified by conditional and unconditional transfer instructions (e.g., JUMP and CALL).

Programmed I/O - Another term for Direct I/O.

Programmed Operator - Another term for a Service Call.

Protection - A system mechanism that prevents one task from interfering with the execution of another task.

Protection Domain - A task protection environment defined by the currently active capability segment(s).

Protection Violation - An attempt by a software module to access a protected resource (especially the memory reserved for another module) or to perform an unauthorized operation on an assigned resource. Examples of operations that generate protection violations are: attempting to write a *read only* file, attempting to delete a file belonging to another user, or attempting to execute a privileged instruction in the user mode.

Protocol - The rules by which messages (containing information) are transmitted between computer systems. A protocol specifies interface voltage levels, message formats and contents, and error recovery techniques.

PSW - An abbreviation for Processor Status Word.

Queue - A data structure in which the first element in is the first element out; this data structure works in the same manner as a supermarket checkout line.

Ready - A signal used by a peripheral device or memory subsystem to indicate that the peripheral or memory is ready to accept or transfer information.

Real Time Clock - A system clock that indicates actual

elapsed time from some reference time (e.g., midnight).

Recursive - A procedure that calls itself either directly or indirectly (through another procedure).

Reentrant - Code that may be executed simultaneously by more than one software module (task). Reentrant code cannot be self-modifying and each software module must maintain its own data area.

Register - A high speed storage location associated with a processor. Registers are normally used to store intermediate data and addresses within a program (to decrease execution time). Due to the high speed requirements and cost, the number of registers within a processor is usually limited to 8 or 16 storage locations, although some processsors have hundreds.

Register Addressing - An addressing mode in which the effective address of one or both of the operands is a register designation. Register addressing reduces instruction length; addressing 16 registers in an instruction requires 4 bits of address information while a complete memory address needs 12-24 bits. Register addressing is often specified in combination with general memory addresses in two-address instructions. This combination permits operations to take place between arbitrary memory locations and one of the processor registers.

Register Set - The group of registers that a program can access through the register addressing mode. Many system architectures include multiple register sets to support fast interrupt service and context switching. Normally, special instructions are provided in the instruction set to select the required register set.

Relative Addressing - An addressing mode that permits addresses to be specified relative to the address of the current instruction (program counter). This mode is normally implemented by including a small (6 to 16 bit) signed offset field in the instruction code. This count is added to the current contents of the program counter in order to obtain the effective address for the instruction. Relative addressing has two distinct features: relative address instructions are shorter than direct address instructions and position independent code is obtained when relative transfer instructions (e.g., JUMP and CALL) are utilized throughout a software module.

Relocatable Code - The output of language translators that contains instruction templates and symbolic addressing tables. A linking loader translates these instruction templates (including address references) into machine instructions that will properly execute at the specified load address.

Relocation - The process of changing the location of a program in system memory. Relocation may either be static or dynamic. With static relocation, all program addresses are assigned and fixed before the program is loaded into memory. Dynamic relocation refers to a technique that requires all program addresses to be relative to some base address and programs may be relocated at any time by moving the program code and changing the base address.

Replacement Policy - The algorithm used by the system to load a page or segment into an already filled memory. The replacement algorithm determines pages or segments that must be removed from memory in order to load the new page/segment.

Representation - The manner in which information is coded within a computer system.

Request - A signal or message used by either a hardware or software system component to indicate the need for a system resource. For example, processors may request the system bus, while tasks may request input from an I/O device.

Resource - An asset of a computer system that can be allocated to a task. Typical system resources are primary and secondary memory space, printers, terminals, and processors.

Resource Sharing - The ability of a distributed processing system to share expensive peripherals (such as printers and disk drives) among many systems by means of a high-speed communication network.

Responder - A content-addressable memory word in which a match occurs.

Return Address - The address of the next instruction to be executed at the completion of a procedure. The return address is normally the address of the instruction (in the calling program) immediately following the procedure call.

Ring - A communication network configuration in which all devices are connected to the network manager in a loop arrangement. Messages from the network manager must pass through each prior device in the loop before reaching the assigned destination.

Root - The source (top) node of a tree data structure.

Scheduler - A system function that determines which task within the system should be executed next.

Secondary Storage - Data storage that is not randomly addressable, is too slow for direct access, or must be accessed in fixed size blocks. Disks, bubble memories, and LCS are examples of secondary storage.

Sector - The smallest addressable contiguous storage area on a magnetic storage medium. In microprocessor systems with flexible disk drives as the secondary storage, a sector is typically between 128 bytes and 4096 bytes in length.

Segment - An arbitrary user defined block (of data or instructions) that functions as an independent unit. A segment may be placed anywhere in memory and its contents accessed by segment name and relative location within the segment. Some computer systems implement segmentation in hardware by means of a Base Register (to contain the starting address of the segment), with all segment accesses occurring relative to the segment starting address.

Segment Descriptor - An element within the segment table that contains the base address for a segment.

Segment Table - A table of segment descriptors for all segments of a task. The segment table is used for memory allocation, relocation, and paging.

Selector Channel - An I/O channel used in conjunction with high-speed I/O devices such as disk drives. Although more than one device may be attached to a selector channel, the channel can service only one device at a time.

Self-Modifying Code - A section of computer instructions whose execution has, as one of its effects, the modification of one or more of the instructions within that section. Self-modifying code cannot be stored in ROM/PROM and self-modifying code is not re-entrant.

Semaphore - A "gating" variable used to synchronize task operations on a shared resource. A semaphore permits only a single task to access a shared resource at any given time — all other tasks are locked out until the first task completes its access.

Send - A system communication and synchronization primitive that permits a task to place a message in another task's mailbox.

Serial - 1) The processing of instructions one at a time. 2) A data link over which data is transmitted one bit at a time.

Serially Reusable Resource - A resource that may be used by another task as soon as the current task is finished using the resource. Printers and CRT terminals are serially reusable resources.

Service Call - A task request for a hardware or operating system service such as timekeeping, memory allocation, or I/O.

Shared Data - Data in memory or on a secondary storage device that is used by more than one task.

Sign-Magnitude - A numeric representation in which a number is stored in two distinct portions, a sign (positive or negative) and an absolute magnitude.

SIMD - An abbreviation for Single Instruction stream, Multiple Data stream. In this architecture, parallel ALUs operate on multiple data elements simultaneously under the control of a single instruction (e.g., vector addition).

Simplex - A data link that can transmit information in only one direction.

SISD - An abbreviation for Single Instruction stream, Single Data stream. A processor in which a single ALU performs one instruction at a time and operates on one data element at a time.

Slave - A unit that responds to communication system commands.

Slave Processor - Another term for a Coprocessor.

Soft Error - A dynamic error normally caused by a transient condition. Retrying the failed operation will often result in successful completion.

Spooling - An I/O technique that permits I/O transfer requests to be queued for an I/O device, permitting tasks to continue executing even when an I/O device is not free. Spooling techniques are generally used with slow sequential output devices such as printers.

Stack - A data structure that operates in the same manner as a cafeteria cup or plate dispenser. New items are added to the top of the existing stack and old items are automatically pushed down in the stack. Items may only be removed from the top of the stack (all other items are "below the counter"). The last item put on the stack is always the first one off (LIFO - last-in first-out). The stack expands or contracts as information is added or removed. In actual implementations, a data area in memory is reserved for the stack and a register (Stack Pointer) contains the memory address of the top of the stack. Instructions are provided to save data in the stack (PUSH onto the stack) and remove data from the stack (POP off the stack). Many processors utilize stacks for subroutine linkages. In addition, some architectures utilize stacks for computations in the same manner as a Reverse Polish Notation (RPN) calculator.

Stack Pointer (SP) - A register that contains the address of the current top-of-stack. This register is modified (incremented or decremented) whenever items are added to, or removed from, the stack.

Star - A type of communications network configuration in which all devices are connected directly to a single network manager (often a minicomputer). Communication lines emanate from the network manager in a star-like shape. Each device communicates only with the network manager.

Store and Forward - A data communication strategy in which nodes temporarily store and subsequently retransmit messages or packets of information as the messages proceed through the network.

Stored Program Computer - A computer system in which the control algorithm (program) is stored in memory within the system.

Streaming Tape - A high density tape unit used to archive the contents of sealed, non-removable disk drives.

String - A sequence of character codes stored sequentially in memory.

Subroutine - A procedure with a well-defined beginning (entry point) and end (exit point).

Supervisor State - Another term for the Privileged Mode.

Swapping - A system feature that permits suspended tasks to be moved to secondary storage in order to release enough primary storage space so that another task can be loaded into memory and executed. The swapped task will be moved back into system memory when it is scheduled to resume execution. This movement to and from secondary storage may occur many times to a given task before its execution is complete.

Symbolic Addressing - A segmented addressing technique in which the effective address calculation cannot alter the segment number.

Synchronization - The process of coordinating task execution within a computer system.

Synchronous - A communication technique that forces both the transmitter and receiver to operate from the same data clock.

System Mode - Another term for Privileged Mode.

Tag - Information stored with each data element or data structure that enables a processor to correctly address and operate on the data. Tags often specify data type, size, and structure.

Tagged Data - A non-Von Neumann architectural design in which a tag (specifying data access and use information) is stored with each data element and/or data structure.

Task - The combination of a program (sequence of instructions) and a context (state information) that is executed by a processor in a sequential manner.

Thrashing - The point of system collapse in which system overhead is so large that no useful task execution can be accomplished. Thrashing occurs often in virtual storage systems when so many tasks are executing that every time the system attempts to service a user, a page fault occurs, and the system is constantly attempting to load/reload pages from secondary storage.

Three-Address Instruction - An instruction that contains three addresses: the addresses of the two operands and the address in which the result is to be stored. The address of the next instruction is not explicitly specified; the next instruction is assumed to begin at the address immediately following that of the current instruction.

Throughput - The quantity of information processed by a computer system in a unit time. This quantity is frequently used for system comparisons.

Tightly Coupled - A multiprocessor configuration in which all processors operate under the direction of a single operating system and share access to the same memory units and peripheral devices. If the processors within a tightly coupled system are identical, load sharing can be performed. Load sharing permits a ready-to-run software module to be executed by any free processor; in fact, execution of the module may move from one processor to another as execution is interrupted and other processors become free.

Time Multiplexing - A technique used to maximize the effective bandwidth of a communication channel and minimize the number of signal lines by using a single channel for more than one purpose at different times.

Timer - A hardware device that supplies interrupts on an interval or time-of-day basis to the operating system.

Time Sharing - A type of computer system that supports more than one user concurrently, and allows each user to interact with his job. Time sharing systems allocate processors and resources to each user (in turn) for a small period of time, ensuring each user a system response within a few seconds.

Time Slice - That period of time, normally 1-50 milliseconds, allocated to each task in a time sharing system.

Track - The storage area on a rotating secondary storage medium (such as a disk drive) defined by one complete revolution of the medium with no head movement. In microprocessor systems using an IBM standard soft-sectored single density diskette, a track is 26 sectors, or 3328 data bytes.

Tree - A data structure that is used to implement hierarchical information relationships.

Two-Address Instruction - An instruction that contains two operand addresses. The operation specified by the instruction (e.g., add or subtract) is performed using the data from both addresses. The result of the computation replaces the data at one of the addresses. The address of the next instruction is not explicitly specified; the next instruction is assumed to begin at the address immediately following that of the current instruction. Two-Address instructions are prevalent in today's computer architectures. One address is often restricted to designate a register (in order to shorten instruction length).

Twos Complement - A common representation technique employed to code signed integers within a computer system.

Type - A data representation. Integer, floating point, and fixed point numbers, character strings, and boolean values are examples of data types.

Unary - Another term for Monadic.

User Mode - A mode of processor operation in which privileged instructions may not be executed. User application software normally executes in the user mode; operating system software executes in the Privileged Mode.

User Profile - A system maintained table or file of information containing user capabilities, access rights, privileges, and passwords.

Vector - A linear data structure in which each element is referenced by the vector name or base address and an index. The index is an integer between 0 and the maximum number of elements in the vector.

Vectored Interrupt - A method of interrupt processing in which each interrupt is given a number (0-n). When an interrupt is acknowledged, this number is used as an index to an interrupt service routine address list (vector of addresses). The processor transfers execution control to the address contained in the interrupt vector.

Vertical Microcode - A method of control storage design that reduces microinstruction width by decreasing the number of functions that can be performed simultaneously. A vertical microprogram storage organization trades off microinstruction width and expense against microprogram length and speed of execution.

Vertical Redundancy Check (VRC) - An error detection method that applies a check procedure against each character or word of transmitted/stored data. Normally a single parity bit is added to each data element. This bit is checked whenever the data element is read or received (over a data link).

Virtual Memory - A memory addressing technique that separates the logical address space from the physical address space. This separation permits an application program to be written and executed independent of the available physical memory. The logical address space may be larger, the same size, or smaller than the physical memory space. Normally the logical address space is far larger, automatically accessing a disk or drum for storage that cannot be contained in physical memory.

Virtual Processor - A logical processor dedicated to the execution of a single task. Each task has its own virtual processor; physical processors within the system are sequentially shared by competing virtual processors. The state of the virtual processor at any time is contained within the task's context.

Virtual Storage - Another term for Virtual Memory.

Volume - A unit of secondary storage media such as a magnetic tape, disk pack, or flexible diskette.

Von-Neumann Architecture - The architecture of a computer system in which both programs and data are stored in a single sequential and linear (one-dimensional) memory. A Von-Neumann architecture recognizes no inherent distinction between program code and data values stored in memory or between data types and their representations.

Voting - A system error detection technique in which three or more processors perform the same computations and compare results. If a single processor's results do not agree with the others, the processor is outvoted and declared inoperative.

Wait - A communication and synchronization primitive that causes a task to wait at a mailbox for the next message. If a message is currently in the mailbox, the task receives the message and continues executing.

Word - A data element (consisting of more than one data bit) that is treated as a single quantity by a computer system. Words are generally 8, 16, 32, or 64 bits, although 4- and 12-bit words are common for some microprocessors.

Working Register Set - The group of registers that can be accessed by a program as it executes. Many machines have multiple register sets, only one of which can be used at a time.

Working Set - That set of pages in a virtual memory system which a given task references in a specified period of time. In order to execute a task without page faults, its working set must be in memory when it is restarted.

Writeable Control Store (WCS) - Microprogram storage designed with high-speed RAM memory in a microprogrammed processor architecture. A writeable control store permits the instruction set of a processor to be easily modified. One important use of a writeable control store is during the processor design and microprogram development stage of a project. In production, a writeable control store permits the development of instruction sets customized to high level languages (e.g., FORTRAN and COBOL). This customized instruction set eases the task of language translators and results in faster program execution.

Zero-Address Instruction - An instruction that contains no addressing information. Control instructions (e.g., HALT, ENABLE INTERRUPTS, NO-OP) are often of this type. Zero-address arithmetic and logic instructions implicitly use the accumulator or the stack as the location of the operand(s). The results of the operation are stored back into the accumulator or the stack. The address of the next instruction is not explicitly specified; the next instruction is assumed to begin at the address immediately following that of the current instruction.

Appendix B

References

AMD, <u>Build A Microcomputer</u>, Advanced Micro Devices, California, 1978.

Bell, C. G., J. C. Mudge, and J. E. McNamara, <u>Computer Engineering</u>, Digital Press, Massachusetts, 1978.

Foster, C. C., <u>Computer Architecture</u>, Van Nostrand Reinhold, New York, 1970.

Foster, C. C., <u>Content Addressable Parallel Processors</u>, Van Nostrand Reinhold, New York, 1976.

Hamming, R. W., <u>Coding and Information Theory</u>, Prentice-Hall, New Jersey, 1980.

Hayes, J. P., <u>Computer Architecture and Organization</u>, McGraw-Hill, New York, 1978.

Husson, S. S., *Microprogramming: Principles and Practices*, Prentice-Hall, New Jersey, 1970.

IBM, *IBM System/38 Technical Developments*, IBM GSD Technical Communications, Georgia, 1978.

Intel, *Microsystem 80 Advance Information*, Intel, 1980.

Myers, G. J., *Advances in Computer Architecture*, John Wiley & Sons, New York, 1978.

National Semiconductor, *The NS 16000 Family of 16-bit Microprocessors: Family Overview*, National Semiconductor, 1980.

Salisbury, A. B., *Microprogrammable Computer Architecture*, Elsevier North Holland, New York, 1976.

Tanenbaum, A. S., *Structured Computer Organization*, Prentice-Hall, New Jersey, 1976.

Watson, R. W., *Time Sharing System Design Concepts*, McGraw-Hill, 1970.

Wilkes, M. V., and R. M. Needham, *The Cambridge CAP Computer and Its Operating System*, Elsevier North Holland, New York, 1979.

Wilkes, M. V., *Time Sharing Computer Systems*, American Elsevier, New York, 1975.

Zilog, *An Introduction to the Z8010 MMU Memory Management Unit*, Zilog, California, 1979.

INDEX

Absolute Addressing, 73
Absolute Code, 62
Accept, 89
Access List, 66
Access Path, 129
Access Rights, 57, 126
Accumulator, 24
Address, 60
Address Map, 61
Addressing Mode, 72
Allocation, 118
Algorithm, 2
Architecture, 2, 15
Argument, 30
Arithmetic-Logic Unit (ALU), 11, 156
Array, 53-54
Array Processor, 105
ASCII, 20
Associative Memory, 109
Asynchronous, 94
Attached Processor, 148
Back-End Processor, 148
Backplane, 81
Bank Switching, 14
Base Register, 63
Baud, 94
BCD, 44
Best Fit, 120
Binary, 25, 42
Binding, 62
Bit, 20
Bit Map, 122
Bit Slice, 156
Block, 70
Block Check Character (BCC), 167
Branch, 29, 54
Bubble Memory, 146-148
Buffer Memory, 139
Bus, 80, 81-85
Bus Interface Unit, 162
Busy Wait, 88
Byte, 20
Cache, 60
Call, 30
Calling Program, 30
Calling Sequence, 31
Capability, 132
Capability Segment, 132
Card Cage, 82
Carry Lookahead, 158
Central Processing Unit (CPU), 10
Chaining, 139
Character, 20
Checkpoint, 115
Communication, 85-89, 95-99
Communication Primitives, 80, 88
Concentrator, 138, 148
Consumable Resource, 118, 119
Consumer, 118
Content-Addressable Memory, 109
Context, 12, 41
Control Store, 150
Coprocessor, 106
Coroutine, 32
Critical Section, 87
Cycle Stealing, 139
Cyclic Redundancy Check (CRC), 168
Daisy Chain, 81; 97
Data, 20
Data Link, 91

Data Stream, 102
Data Structure, 40, 48
    array, 53-54
    linked list, 49
    queue, 51-53
    tree, 54-56
    vector, 53-54
Data Types
    integer, 43-44
    fixed point, 45
    floating point, 45-46
    logic, 46
    string, 47
Decision Tree, 56
Demand Paging, 70
Device Driver, 140
Direct Addressing, 73
Direct I/O, 136
Directory, 76
Dirty Bit, 124
Dispatcher, 12
Distributed Intelligence, 112
Distributed Processing, 11, 102, 112
DMA, 138, 161-162
Dual Port Memory, 139
Dyadic, 25
EBCDIC, 20
Effective Address, 72
Emulation, 153
Entry Point, 12, 31
Error Correcting Code, 169
Event, 172
Event Flag, 87
Exception, 172
Execute Cycle, 40
Exit Point, 31
Extended Addressing, 14

Extended Processing Unit (EPU), 106
Fault, 164
Fault Avoidance, 164
Fault Detection, 164
Fault Tolerant, 115, 164
Fetch Cycle, 40
File, 76
First Fit, 120
First-In First-Out (FIFO), 124
Fixed Point, 45
Floating Point, 45-46
Format, 143
Four-Address Instruction, 23
Fragmentation, 120
Friendly Environment, 126
Front-End Processor, 148
Full Duplex, 94
Garbage Collection, 120, 122
Gate, 130
Generalized Address, 64
GPIB, 95
Graceful Degradation, 115
Half Duplex, 94
Hamming Code, 169
Hardwired, 3
Horizontal Microcode, 153-155
Huffman Coding, 36
IEEE-488, 95
Immediate Addressing, 72
Index Register, 75
Indexed Addressing, 75
Indirect Addressing, 73
Indirect I/O, 137
Input, 136
Instruction, 12, 21, 23, 24, 25, 28, 129

Instruction Pointer, 23
Instruction Prefix, 36
Instruction Set, 21
Instruction Stream, 102
Integer, 43-44
Interleaving, 146
Interleave Factor, 146
Interrupt, 4, 80, 89-91, 160
Interrupt Latency, 90
Interrupt Vector, 91
Intersegment Reference, 64
I/O, 10
I/O Channel, 109, 137
I/O Interface, 136
I/O Mapped, 136
I/O Processor, 4, 109, 137
Job, 12
Known Segment Table, 66
Least Recently Used, 124
Line Switching, 98-99
Line Turnaround Time, 94
Linear Addressing, 72
Link, 49
Linkage Segment, 66
Linked List, 49
Linking Loader, 62
Load Sharing, 107-108
Logical Address, 13, 60
Logical Address Space, 13
Longitudinal Redundancy Check (LRC), 169
Looping, 29
Loosely Coupled, 108
Machine Level Interrupt, 161
Macroinstruction, 150
Mailbox, 87, 88-89
Master, 80, 81-82
Memory Mapped, 85, 136
Message, 85-86
Microcycle, 151
Microinstruction, 150
Microprocessor, 5
Microprogram, 150
Microprogrammed Processor, 5
Microprogram Sequencer, 160
MIMD, 102
MISD, 102
Module, 29
Monadic, 25
Multidrop, 97
Multiplexed Bus, 83-84
Multiplexer, 148
Multiplexer Channel, 138
Multiport Memory, 82
Multiprocessing, 107
Multiprogramming, 12, 41
Multitasking, 12, 41
Nesting Depth, 31
Network, 95
Nibble, 20
Node, 54, 95
Non-Von Neumann Architecture, 17
Object, 18, 40, 48
Object-Addressing, 48
One-Address Instruction, 25
One-Level Store, 77
Op Code, 22
Operand, 22
Operating System, 3
Operation Code, 22
Output, 136
Packet Switching, 32, 98-99

Page, 69
Page Fault, 70
Page Frame, 70
Page Table, 70
Paging, 69, 123
Parallel, 80, 93, 102
Parallel Processing, 11
Parameter, 30
Parity
PC Relative Addressing, 72
Peripheral Processing Unit (PPU), 137
Physical Address, 13, 60
Physical Address Space, 13
Pipelining, 103-105, 151
Pointer, 56
Polling, 89
Pool, 119
Position Independent Code, 64
Prefetching, 105
Primary Store, 61
Privileged Instruction, 24, 129
Privileged Mode, 129
Procedure, 18, 29
Process, 12
Processor, 11, 40
Processor Status Word (PSW), 40
Producer, 118
Program, 3, 12, 20
Program Counter (PC), 23
Programmed I/O, 136
Programmed Operator, 130
Protection, 118, 126, 127, 130
Protection Domain, 132-133

Protection Violation, 127
Protocol, 91
Queue, 51-53, 88
Recursive, 33
Reentrant, 33
Register, 11, 24
Relocatable Code, 62
Relocation, 62
Replacement Policy, 123-124
Representation, 40
Resource, 118, 119
Resource Sharing, 112
Responder, 109
Return Address, 31
Ring, 97
Root, 54
Scheduler, 12
Secondary Storage, 61
Sector, 143
Segment, 62
Segment Descriptor, 66
Segment Table, 66
Selector Channel, 138
Self-Modifying Code, 33
Semaphore, 80, 87-88
Send, 88
Serial, 11, 80, 93, 102
Serially Reusable Resource, 118
Service Call, 130
SIMD, 102
Simplex, 94
SISD, 102
Slave, 80, 81
Slave Processor, 106
Spooling, 140
Stack, 33, 49-51
Star, 95
Store and Forward, 99

Stored Program Computer, 3
Streaming Tape, 148
String, 47
Subroutine, 31
Swapping, 63
Symbolic Addressing, 72
Synchronization, 87
Synchronous, 93
Tag, 26
Tagged Data, 26
Task, 12, 41
Thrashing, 124, 125
Three-Address Instruction, 23
Tightly Coupled, 107
Time Multiplexing, 83-84
Track, 143
Tree, 54-56
Two-Address Instruction, 24
Type (See Data Type)
Unary, 25
User Mode, 129
User Profile, 133
Vector, 53-54
Vectored Interrupt, 91
Vertical Microcode, 153-155
Vertical Redundancy Check (VRC), 167
Virtual Memory, 14
Virtual Processor, 41
Virtual Storage, 14
Volume, 76
Von-Neumann Architecture, 10
Voting, 115
Wait, 88
Word, 20
Working Set, 125
Writeable Control Store (WCS), 155
Zero-Address Instruction, 24